FLOWER GARDENING — IN 7 SIMPLE STEPS

BEGINNER'S GUIDE TO GARDEN DESIGN DISCOVER
HOW TO GROW AND MAINTAIN YOUR HOME FLOWER
GARDEN YEAR ROUND

SANDY NEWTON

CONTENTS

Introduction   7

1. STEP 1- BECOME FAMILIAR WITH   13
   YOUR ZONE
   Getting to Know Your Climate   13
   Understanding the Different Hardiness   18
   Zones in the Plant Map
   How to Choose Cold-Hardy Plants for   36
   Your Zone

2. STEP 2- TEST YOUR SOIL   39
   Determining Your Soil Type   42
   Improving Soil Drainage   45
   Soil pH   48

3. STEP 3- DETERMINE YOUR SUN AND   55
   WIND EXPOSURE
   Monitor the Sunlight   56
   Wind Exposure and Wind-Resistant   61
   Plants

4. STEP 4- PLANNING AND PLANTING   71
   ACCORDING TO SPACE
   The Right Path to Spacing   72
   Creating Your Planting Sections   73
   Consider Full-Grown Plants When   75
   Spacing
   Use Graph Paper to Map Out the Garden   77
   Popular Perennials for Spacing   78
   Requirements
   Growing and Caring for Seeds and Bulbs   82
   Annuals   90

5. STEP 5- FEEDING YOUR GARDEN   93
   Composting   93
   Irrigation   100
   Fertilizing   118

6. STEP 6- PROTECTING YOUR GARDEN   127
   Diseases   127
   Pests   143
   Pesticides   154

7. STEP 7- SEASONAL TASKS AND   161
   MAINTENANCE
   Spring Tasks and Spring Blooms   161
   Summer Tasks and Summer Blooms   168
   Autumn Tasks and Autumn Blooms   172
   Winter Tasks and Winter Blooms   176

   Conclusion   183
   References   185

A Special Gift To Our Readers

Included with your purchase of this book is our
Guide to Test your Garden Soil.

This guide will help you determine your soil type
and includes some tricks to improve your soil
drainage if need be.

Scan the Qr code below and let us know which
email address to deliver it to.

INTRODUCTION

All beautiful gardens are a product of gardeners' love and care. When you walk into a well-groomed flower garden, it is often difficult to see the hard work and effort expended to create it. People only see the rewards of following proper garden rules. Healthy flower gardens provide a good spot for playing, resting, and observing nature.

Many people create fantasies about having a healthy garden full of colorful flowers. Of course, it is worth dreaming about considering a large percentage of the population love flowers and spend good money buying roses, petunias, etc.

Those who set up and nurture their own flower garden quickly find satisfaction in its beauty. If you are passionate about colorful flowers, you can set up a flower garden, too. The size of the garden does not matter. You can enjoy doing what you love even if the space around your home is small. All you need is to designate the best spot suitable for the growth of the flowers you are interested in.

However, there's a problem with fulfilling this dream of flower gardening. Many people who are interested in growing beautiful gardens and are thrilled about the idea, nurse a deep-seated fear that flower gardening is too delicate for them to venture into. There are ups and downs, no doubt, certain practices to follow or avoid, and it might be confusing at the beginning.

Beginners to gardening often have many questions plaguing them. What if my flowers die before they bloom? What do I feed my flowers to make them grow? Do I grow them like normal plants? What does flower gardening really involve? What do I do to my plants during winter?

Asking questions like this is evidence that you genuinely want to pour your heart and soul into making this work.

If you have already decided to start gardening, chances are you have no prior knowledge, and you're somewhat at a loss about how to start. You're probably wondering what proper steps to follow to ensure your flower garden blooms as beautifully as you desire.

It's okay to have fears and reservations about starting something new and as delicate as gardening. However, you will begin to enjoy this new journey

with proper guidance.

This book aims to help you build and maintain your dream garden and prevent you from making many of the mistakes that most beginners make.

In this book, you'll learn the basics of gardening from an individual who has successfully created their garden and studied gardening design for the past eight years. All of the chapters of this book have been written based on extensive research and practical trial and error.

Yes, they were trials and errors that I encountered when I was just a beginner like you trying to create my own garden. Since the desire to succeed at flower gardening was so strong, I decided to study garden design, and I have been at it for eight long years.

During my beginner days, I made many mistakes that would have been avoided if I had had resources and books such as this one to guide me. My failures only pushed me toward acquiring more knowledge and ideas on flower gardening. Since I'm passionate about this, I have decided to share everything I've learned in the past eight years with you.

As a beginner, you do not have to make all the frustrating mistakes common with novices. I'm here to help you navigate your way into the world of flower gardening with ease.

This book shares practical and helpful advice on gardening. All the chapters are written in detail to inform and educate.

There are many things to consider when gardening, like the choice of plants, nutrition, fertilizer, weeding, etc. However, some factors contribute to plant growth which can often be ignored by gardening beginners.

Yes, you have to buy fertilizers and plant your flowers in fertile soil, but that's not all there is to it. This book breaks down important gardening topics like climate and zoning maps to help people understand that it is one of the first few things to consider when planting. Climate plays an essential role in the growth of every plant. Not knowing the best flowers to grow in the environment you live in may be the first ingredient in the recipe for gardening failure.

The book also highlights other plant necessities like sun exposure; you must know the sun requirements for the flowers you intend to grow. After learning about plant sunlight requirements in this book, you can design your garden in a way that considers this factor.

The growth of plants is largely affected by wind. For a beginner, it is often challenging to deal with wind interference on young flowers. You will learn helpful tips and ways to deal with wind interference in your garden.

This book also shares valuable tips about plant spacing. Some plants need to have a particular distance between them and others. Find out how to determine the amount of space your plant needs to grow.

While you need to do a lot of research before you start gardening, this book was written to gather practical information that will be immensely helpful to beginners in the world of flower gardening. It exposes you to more information that you probably didn't think you needed and makes your research easier.

Every day, we learn something new, and although this book was tailored to suit beginners, it can also come in handy for gardening experts and people who have been practicing for years. Read through, and you'll learn something new or get a reminder of some gardening tips you've probably forgotten.

This book is your best bet if you're genuinely interested in making the flower garden of your dreams.

1

STEP 1- BECOME FAMILIAR WITH YOUR ZONE

GETTING TO KNOW YOUR CLIMATE

Climate is simply the average weather condition of a particular area over time. The performance of plants is heavily dependent on many climatic factors like rainfall, humidity, wind, summer, or winter.

Every gardener must understand the different types of climates before starting, as it makes the process of gardening an easier task.

The major climate types include tropical climates (hot and humid); dry climate zones (hot and dry); continental (warm/cool summers and very cold winters); temperate zones (warm, wet summers and mild winters); and polar zones (extreme cold winter, cold summer).

Gardeners that plant based on climate zones only concentrate on growing plants that thrive in their gardening climates. If you are interested in growing only zone-specific plants, you'll need to determine your climate and climate zone accurately. This can be done with the aid of climate zone maps. There are also plant hardiness zone maps available for gardeners in the U.S.

The plant hardiness zone maps are tools for gardeners to determine the survival chances of their plants when planted outdoors in their region. Many nurseries indicate the hardiness range of plants to help gardeners choose the right plants for their gardens.

While cold hardiness may be the most common factor being considered when using the plant hardiness zone map, it shouldn't be the only one. As a gardener, you also need to check for the rainfall, temperature during summer, humidity, and how long the growing seasons last.

The climate zones were developed to cater to those factors and help gardeners who intend to start planting in their backyards. While the climate zones provide information about plant hardiness, most people may not quite understand what the term means.

Plant Hardiness

Plant hardiness describes plants' ability to withstand harsh climates like cold, drought, flooding, and heat. The genetics of the plants confer on them their ability to survive in harsh circumstances without being ruined. The different cultivars of a particular plant do not usually share the same hardiness level because of differences in their genetics and adaptations. In some cases, other parts of a plant may have different hardiness levels. For instance, your perennial plant dies from the excess cold, but its roots remain hardy enough to regrow in the following spring.

A lot of plants need a particular environment to grow. Based on plant requirements, it's easy to control soil type, level of moisture, and sunlight levels, but the temperature is often out of reach. Knowing the hardiness level of plants helps you choose plants with temperature requirements that you can work with, which in turn facilitates your gardening success.

Plant Hardiness Zones

The plant hardiness zones keep gardeners from making avoidable mistakes. For instance, if you live in a zone that does not support the growth of oranges, all efforts to grow oranges in your garden will be frustrated. Plant hardiness refers to the temperature range suitable for their development. Therefore, it is crucial to use the hardiness zones as a guide for your garden because it streamlines your choices. While you study the hardiness of the plants you're interested in, understand that plants which are hardy to particular zones will also be hardy to zone numbers higher than that. Based on this, plants hardy in Zone 4 can also do well in Zone 7.

The Hardiness Zone Maps

According to the hardiness zone map, the United States is divided into 13 zones. Each zone categorizes different areas with a focus on the lowest average temperature.

The 2012 USDA Plant Hardiness Zone Map

The United States Department of Agriculture has developed a few zone maps in the past. This 2012 version is the latest and is the product of a joint effort by the USDA's Agricultural Research Service (ARS) and Oregon State University's (OSU) PRISM Climate Group. USDA and OSU, during the process of the map creation, implored experts in climate and horticulture to review the zones they occupy. The expert suggestions they made facilitated the creation of this version of the zone map.

The 2012 version of the zone map adjusts the boundaries that were previously established in the 1990 version. It is also around 5 °F and a half-zone warmer than earlier versions. This is because of the changes in the temperature data range. The 2012 map collects data measurements from weather stations between 1976–2005, a lengthy period of 30 years, unlike the 1990 map that focused on temperature data from the 13 years of 1974–1986 ("USDA Plant Hardiness Zone Map," n.d.).

The changes are also influenced by the modern methods that weather stations currently use to map zones. Some of the new algorithms considered previously overlooked factors like elevation changes, position on terrains, distance to large bodies of water, etc.

This map upgrade compiled temperature data from many more weather stations than the 1990 map. All of these contributed to the accuracy of the recent version.

The 1990 USDA Plant Hardiness Zone Map

The USDA Plant Hardiness Zone Map was the most popular among gardeners, catalogs, books, national garden magazines, nurseries, and websites. Some still use it today. The 1990 zone map divides North America into 11 zones and makes every zone 10 °F warmer (colder) in winter than the adjacent zone.

The 1990 map had several problems. It did not register the benefits that perennial plants derived from snow covers, the frequency of freeze-thaw cycles, and the soil drainage in cold periods that characterized the eastern part of the country. The map also does not accurately describe the climate situation in the West (Meyer, 2021).

UNDERSTANDING THE DIFFERENT HARDINESS ZONES IN THE PLANT MAP

Planting Zone 1

USDA Plant Hardiness Zone 1 is a region of extreme cold. The temperature range is between -60 to -50 degrees °F, which is not so favorable for gardening. Zone 1 is mainly found in Alaska. Zone 1 is a tundra region with extreme weather, and plants need to be extremely cold, hardy, and drought-tolerant to grow there (BH&G Garden Editors, 2020b).

The temperature in Zone 1

- **Zone 1**: The lowest average temperature is from -60 to -50 °F.
- **Zone 1a**: The lowest average temperature is from -60 to -55 °F.
- **Zone 1b:** The lowest average temperature is from -55 to -50 °F.

Note: The weather can trigger harsher temperatures in the subzones.

Plants That Thrive in Zone 1

Growing in Zone 1 is tasking. It is rare to find plants that thrive in the tundra. Although the native plants can do well since it's their natural abode, you can fit in some annuals that are not required to live past the winter. Finding non-native perennials for Zone 1 is a Herculean task, although some can thrive with proper management.

Flowers to Grow in Zone 1

Select only extremely cold, hardy, and drought-tolerant flowers for Zone 1:

- Arrowhead
- Delphinium
- Goldenrod
- Sunflower
- Lily of the valley
- Oxeye daisy
- Yarrow

Planting Zone 2

Planting Zone 2 is found in Alaska and the continental United States. This zone is extremely cold. The average lowest temperatures range from -50 to -40 °F. Gardeners have trouble planting in this region due to the high winds and drought. Some gardeners still plant annuals and modify their planting techniques in this region (BH&G Garden Editors, 2020b).

The temperature in Zone 2

- **Zone 2**: The lowest average temperature is from -50 to -40 °F.
- **Zone 2a**: The lowest average temperature is from -50 to -45 °F.
- **Zone 2b**: Lowest average temperature is from -45 to -40 °F.

Note: The weather can trigger harsher temperatures in the subzones.

Plants to Grow in Zone 2

Only plants with high cold hardiness and drought tolerance can grow in Zone 2. Native plants are the best choice for the region. Annuals may thrive, but perennials require extra care.

Flowers to Grow in Zone 2

Native perennials are the best choice for this zone. These flowers are well suited for Zone 2:

- Bleeding heart
- Monkshood
- Penstemon
- Poppy
- Primrose
- Sea holly
- Violet

Planting Zone 3

Zone 3 is located in Alaska, the northern part of the U.S., and areas with high altitudes. The average lowest temperature ranges from -40 to -30 degrees F. Plant growth is often affected by harsh cold, high winds, and low moisture (BH&G Garden Editors, 2020b).

The temperature in Zone 3

- **Zone 3**: The lowest average temperature is from -40 to -30 °F.
- **Zone 3a**: The lowest average temperature is from -40 to -35 °F.
- **Zone 3b**: The lowest average temperature is from -35 to -30 °F.

Note: The weather can trigger harsher temperatures in the subzones.

Plants to Grow in Zone 3

Only plants that have adapted to low temperatures can thrive in Zone 3. The native plants are well adapted all over the zone despite the difference in altitude. The weather restricts vegetables and flowering annuals. However, gardeners can go around it by buying from a greenhouse or starting plant growth indoors.

Flowers to Grow in Zone 3

They include:

- Alpine rock-cress
- Aster
- Blanket flower
- *Liatris* varieties
- Salvia
- Snow-in-summer
- Spurge
- Virginia bluebells
- Wallflower

Planting Zone 4

Planting Zone 4 is made up of the Northern U.S., southern coastal areas of Alaska, and mountainous elevations in the western regions. The lowest average temperatures range from -30 to -20 °F. Planting in Zone 4 is not as laborious, but the bloom periods for flowers and vegetables change due to the short growing season (BH&G Garden Editors, 2020b).

The temperature in Zone 4

- **Zone 4**: The lowest average temperature is from -30 to -20 °F.
- **Zone 4a**: The lowest average temperature is from -30 to -25 °F.
- **Zone 4b**: The lowest average temperature is from -25 to -20 °F.

Note: The weather can trigger harsher temperatures in the subzones.

Plants to Grow in Zone 4

Zone 4 is a cool climate, and only cold-hardy plants can thrive. Starting plants indoors is one way to boycott the short growing season. Certain gardening practices like mulching can preserve the plants.

Flowers to Grow in Zone 4

These are some hardy native perennial flowers you can choose from:

- Coneflower
- Daylily
- Iris
- Phlox
- Plantain lily (*Hosta*)

Planting Zone 5

The southern coastal region of Alaska, the North Central United States, and portions of New England are all grouped under Zone 5. The lowest average temperature range is -20 °F and -10 °F. The winter in this zone is moderate. However, the short growing season can be restrictive for plants. Gardeners should start their plants indoors (BH&G Garden Editors, 2020b).

The temperature in Zone 5

- **Zone 5**: The lowest average temperature is from -20 to -10 °F.
- **Zone 5a**: The lowest average temperature is from -20 to -15 °F.
- **Zone 5b**: The lowest average temperature is

from -15 to -10 °F.

Note: The weather can trigger harsher temperatures in the subzones.

Plants to Grow in Zone 5

Zone 5 has different kinds of environments. Plants to be grown in this zone should be both cold-hardy and suitable for the growing environment. The growing seasons in this zone are longer.

Flowers to Grow in Zone 5

These perennial flowers have the right hardiness needed for survival in Zone 5:

- Baptisia
- Black-eyed Susan
- Campanula
- Cinquefoil
- Russian sage

Planting Zone 6

The majority of the United States falls under USDA Hardiness Zone 6. The climate is mild, and the winter temperatures range lies around -10 to 0 °F. Zone 6 has varying winter and summer experiences with different growing options for gardeners (BH&G Garden Editors,

2020b).

The temperature in Zone 6

- **Zone 6**: The lowest average temperature is from -10 to -0 °F.
- **Zone 6a**: The lowest average temperature is from -10 to -5 °F.
- **Zone 6b**: The lowest average temperature is from -5 to -0 °F.

Note: The weather can trigger harsher temperatures in the subzones.

Plants to Grow in Zone 6

Zone 6 is regarded as the standard for landscaping and gardening. Gardeners find many plant options for this zone in nurseries, garden centers, and seed companies. Planting is possible in fall, spring, and summer.

Flowers to Grow in Zone 6

Zone 6 supports plant (flower) bloom for months. Cold-hardy flowers like pansies and snapdragons can thrive in this region. Also, these other flowers are good:

- False sunflower
- Floribunda rose
- Flowering fern

- Japanese bottlebrush
- Lady's mantle
- Sedum

Planting Zone 7

About 15 states occupy the planting Zone 7 sections. It comprises cool winters, and the lowest temperatures range from 0 to 10 °F. There are many plant options from local home stores, seed catalogs, greenhouses, and nurseries in this zone (BH&G Garden Editors, 2020b).

The temperature in Zone 7

- Zone 7: The lowest average temperatures 0 to 10 °F.
- Zone 7a: The lowest average temperatures 0 to 5 °F.
- Zone 7b: The lowest average temperature of 5 to 10 °F.

Note: The weather can trigger harsher temperatures in the subzones.

Plants to Grow in Zone 7

You can find various growing climates in Zone 7. The eastern coastal areas from the Oklahoma prairies to the dry southwest regions and the Oregon and Washington forests are located in Zone 7. Due to the different climates in this zone, gardeners have to make adjustments to the soil and fit in drought tolerance. Zone 7 hardy plants have the potential to grow in more than one location as long as their specific needs are considered.

Flowers to Grow in Zone 7

Zone 7 favors the growth of many flowering annuals. Gardner's may also include perennials like:

- Butterfly weed
- Candytuft
- Chrysanthemum
- Clematis
- Forget-me-not
- Four o'clock
- Painted daisy
- Peony

Planting Zone 8

Zone 8 is among the warmest plant hardiness zones for most of the Southern United States. Zone 8 stretches up to the western coastal region. The average lowest winter temperatures range between 10 to 20 °F. The mild winters and hot summers in this zone allow for long growing seasons (BH&G Garden Editors, 2020b).

The temperature in Zone 8

- **Zone 8:** The lowest average temperature is from 0 to 10 °F.
- **Zone 8a**: The lowest average temperature is from 0 to 10 °F.
- **Zone 8b:** The lowest average temperature is from 0 to 10 °F.

Note: The weather can trigger harsher temperatures in the subzones.

Plants to Grow in Zone 8

Zone 8 hardy plants thrive in cold winters and long, hot summers. Since plants have different moisture and sunlight requirements, gardeners should recategorize all Zone 8 hardy plants based on their individual growing climates.

Flowers to Grow in Zone 8

Zone 8 hardy flowers need to have the capacity to endure hot summers. Some shade and moisture may be needed on hotter days. These flowers are most suited for some 8:

- Asiatic lily
- Hardy geranium

- Lantana
- Mexican petunia
- Phlox

Planting Zone 9

This is the zone known for all-year planting. Zone 9 is located in Arizona, California, Florida, around the Gulf of Mexico coast, and Texas. The weather condition tilts between warm winters and hot summers. The average lowest winter temperature ranges between 20 to 30 °F. Gardeners in this zone maintain their gardens year-round (BH&G Garden Editors, 2020b).

The temperature in Zone 9

- **Zone 9:** The lowest average temperature is from 20 to 30 °F.
- **Zone 9a:** The lowest average temperature is from 20 to 25 °F.
- **Zone 9b**: The lowest average temperature is from 25 to 30 °F.

Note: The weather can trigger harsher temperatures in the subzones.

Plants to Grow in Zone 9

Zone 9 gardeners have more trouble with the heat than the cold due to the long, hot summers and mild winters. Zone 9 favors the growth of tropical plants with low water needs. The extreme heat causes early spring gardening, and the fall gardens have a longer production time.

Flowers to Grow in Zone 9

Gardens on Zone 9 bloom all year. The mild winters suit the cold-hardy plants, and the tropical perennials thrive during summer.

These flowers are great for zone 9:

- Black-eyed Susan
- Canna
- Dahlia
- Hydrangea
- Rhododendrons
- Wisteria
- Zinnia

Planting Zone 10

Zone 10 is located in Hawaii, Southern (inland) California, and the south of Florida. Here, the average lowest winter temperatures range between 30 to 40 °F.

Zone 10 gardeners enjoy winter gardening because the temperature is fair, but they're greatly limited by the hot summers (BH&G Garden Editors, 2020b).

The temperature in Zone 10

- **Zone 10**: The lowest average temperature is from 30 to 40 °F.
- **Zone 10a**: The lowest average temperature is from 30 to 35 °F.
- **Zone 10b**: The lowest average temperature is from 35 to 40 °F.

Note: The weather can trigger harsher temperatures in the subzones.

Plants That Grow in Zone 10

Zone 10 is the best zone for many tropical plants. Farmers only have to worry about the high heat and humidity during summer, as there are fewer frosts.

Flowers to Grow in Zone 10

Zone 10 is excellent for tropical plants. You can plant flowers like:

- Aeoniums
- Agave
- African lily

- Delta maidenhair fern
- Floss flower
- Geraniums
- Hummingbird mint
- Ornamental onion
- Peruvian lily
- Various aloes

Planting Zone 11

Puerto Rico, the Florida Keys, and some areas of the continental United States make up Zone 11. This zone is extremely warm. Winter is sparse, and the average lowest temperatures are around 40 to 50 °F. Plants that grow in this zone do not need to be cold-hardy. Gardeners here focus on heat tolerance when choosing plants (BH&G Garden Editors, 2020b).

The temperature in Zone 11

- **Zone 11**: The lowest average temperature is from 40 to 50 °F.
- **Zone 11a**: The lowest average temperature is from 40 to 45 °F.
- **Zone 11b**: The lowest average temperature is from 45 to 50 °F.

Note: The weather can trigger harsher temperatures in the subzones.

Plants That Grow in Zone 11

Zone 11 is abundant with tropical plants. The hot, lengthy summers and warm winters make farmers choose heat-tolerant plants. Plants naturally adapted for the cold season will barely thrive here because the winter is not cold enough. The summer heat may be too extreme for foreign plants, but local plants are capable of surviving here.

Flowers to Grow in Zone 11

Cool-season flowers can be grown in zone 11 winters, but they are often unable to survive the extreme heat in summer. These are some heat-tolerant flowers to plant in Zone 11:

- Anemone coronaria
- Begonias
- Bougainvillea
- Drumstick allium
- Kangaroo paw
- Ponytail palm

Planting Zones 12 and 13

Planting zones 12 and 13 are in Hawaii and Puerto Rico outside the continental United States. These zones are very warm and great for plants with intense heat tolerance. The average lowest winter temperature ranges from 50 and 70 °F. This zone is the warmest and harbors exotic fruits and tropical plants (Gardenia, 2021).

Temperatures in Zone 12 and 13

- **Zone 12**: The Lowest average temperature is from 50 to 60 °F.
- **Zone 12a**: The Lowest average temperature is from 50 to 55 °F.
- **Zone 12b**: The lowest average temperature is from 55 to 60 °F.
- **Zone 13**: The lowest average temperature is from 60 to 70 °F.
- **Zone 13a**: The lowest average temperature is from 60 to 65 °F.
- **Zone 13b**: The lowest average temperature is from 65 to 70 °F.

Plants to Grow in Zone 12 and 13

These zones have problems with heat and tropical plants can thrive in the extreme heat. Gardeners can start their plants indoors or buy from nurseries to avoid being affected by the weather.

Flowers to Grow in Zones 12 and 13

Although this is a hot climate, tropical plants will do well with proper care. These flowers thrive in zone 12 and 13:

- *Musaceae*
- *Strelitziaceae*
- *Heliconia*
- *Zingiberaceae*
- *Costaceae*
- *Cannaceae*
- *Marantaceae*
- *Lowiaceae*

HOW TO CHOOSE COLD-HARDY PLANTS FOR YOUR ZONE

As soon as you have figured which zone you're in, find out if your plant is annual or perennial. Compare your zone to those on plant tags.

A plant will be perennial in your area if you live in a zone equal to or higher than the zone listed on the plant tag. For instance, if your home zone is 5. A plant with hardiness for Zones 5–9 is hardy and perennial for your area AND in Zones 6, 7, 8, and 9, but it will not be perennials for you if you live in Zone 4.

A plant cannot be perennial in your area if you live in a zone lower than the listed one.

Although hardiness zones often refer to a plant's ability to survive harsh cold weather, they can also identify if your zone is too warm for a plant. If your zone is too cold for your plant, it dies in winter.

If you plant a cold-hardy plant in a warmer zone, the plant is unlikely to do well. For instance, if plant hardiness places it in Zones 5–9, planting it in Zone 10 will cause it to grow poorly.

Find out your zone, the climate, and how hardiness works, then choose perennial plants accordingly.

It is important to note that the hardiness zone map is based on the assumption that the plants will be grown in the ground and not in containers. The ground is usually warmer and does not freeze solid like containers. Containers thaw out a lot of times, and this thawing and refreezing reduces the hardiness of container-grown perennials. The hardiness zones refer to plants grown in the ground, and if you are planting in a container, choose plants that are hardier by two zones above your current location.

If you live in Zone 5 and choose to plant in containers, go for plants that are hardy to zone 3. Alternatively, you could place the container in a hole in your garden so the surrounding soil keeps it warm during winter.

Due to constant research, newer species of plants may be less hardy or hardier than the normal species. Do not always regard it as a mistake if you find a plant listing a zone that is hardier or less hardy than the general species.

In some cases, you can find a plant zone less hardy than yours thriving in your area as a perennial. This could either be due to incorrect information or some spots in your garden being warmer than average. Typically, areas that have less interference with the wind are warmer. However, it's better to consider the climate and other factors like moisture, drainage, etc., before choosing a plant.

2

STEP 2 - TEST YOUR SOIL

The type of soil in your garden determines how well your plants grow. Most farmers do not know the actual nature of their soil, and some erroneously expect that every soil in its natural state is fertile. Meanwhile, some soils need alterations and significant changes. Finding out your soil condition helps you plan for fertilizers and other adjustments you need to make.

After determining your climate zone, the next thing to find out is the soil type. Scoop up some of the soil in your garden; how does it feel to touch? Does it feel dense and sticky or loose? Is it smooth?

Every soil is a combination of mineral particles— mainly clay, silt, and sand. The difference, however, exists in the fact that the different types of soil have higher quantities of one type of mineral. This eventually affects their drainage and nutrient retention capacity.

Before you start any planting, it is imperative to know which of the six main types of soil yours belong to. Soil can either be sandy, loamy, clay, silty, peaty, and chalky.

Below is a short description to help with the identification (Barton, 2013):

1. **Clay Soil**: It consists of dense and tiny particles with large moisture and nutrient reservoirs. Clay soil feels fine to touch when dry but becomes sticky and lumpy when wet. It does not drain easily and hardens as it dries, usually cracking. This kind of soil is difficult to dig, albeit nutrient-rich.
2. **Sandy Soil**: It is highly porous because it contains large particles. It has poor water retention, which leads to a considerable loss of nutrients. Sandy soil feels gritty and crumbles when touched. It requires extra organic matter and moisture before plants can grow.
3. **Loamy Soil**: It is the standard soil for planting. The three mineral particles are present in a balanced ratio. In addition, loamy soil has

plenty of humus which is excellent for plant growth. Loam has moderate drainage while also being nutrient-rich. This kind of soil can roll into a ball but does not stick or form well.

4. **Silty Soil**: It has fine, tightly packed particles. Although it is porous like sand, it still has some moisture retention capacity and has higher nutrient levels. Just like clay, it feels smooth to touch and can be easily molded; however, it does not retain any shape formed like clay soil.

5. **Chalky Soil**: It is porous, alkaline, and stony. It's usually found as the uppermost layer of a limestone or chalk foundation. Chalky soil can be either light or heavy. This soil type facilitates the leaching of minerals like iron and manganese and will need adjustments before planting.

6. **Peaty Soil**: It has a dark color and feels spongy to the touch. It's acidic, organic matter-rich but nutrient-poor. This type of soil is not a common sight in gardens. Peaty soils retain a lot of moisture, getting waterlogged in many cases. Still, it is helpful for growing acid-loving plants.

DETERMINING YOUR SOIL TYPE

There are different ways to know which category your soil falls into. If visual identification does not work for you, then these are a few tests to determine your garden soil type (Barton, 2013):

The Squeeze Test

Do this test on damp soil, not wet soil. Scoop up a portion of soil in your hand. Use your fingers to feel it. It has more sand if it feels gritty to touch. If it is slimy and greasy, then there's more clay in it.

The Ribbon Test

Scoop some damp soil and roll it between your palms to make a ribbon. If the ribbon forms well and does not break when held vertically, then it is mainly clay soil. If the ribbon can form but breaks when it is held, the soil has between 25–50% clay. If the soil is unable to form a ribbon, then a greater part of it is sand.

The Jar Test

The jar test is more scientific and accurate. For this test, scoop soil from different parts of your garden and combine all the samples in a container.

Follow this procedure:

- Scoop out a cup of the mixed soil and spread it on a flat surface to dry.
- When it's crumbly, sieve out the debris, stone, and roots, and use a mortar to grind it into a powder.
- Get a quart-sized transparent glass jar and line it with a one-inch thick layer of ground soil.
- Pour water to fill two-thirds of the jar, then add a teaspoon of dish soap. This separates the soil particles. Shake the bottle.
- Allow the solution to separate into layers as you observe.

Sand settles faster and sits at the last layer in a few minutes. Silt settles a few hours later. You'll see the difference between the small silt particles and the bigger sand particles on close observation. The clay doesn't settle quickly and may not settle for a day or two.

When all the soil layers have settled, measure the total precipitation. Afterward, measure the different soil layers.

It may be a little complicated because you need to do some math to determine the exact percentage of the different soil types.

For instance, if the soil depth is at one inch and the sand layer has a depth of 1/2 inch, then the soil in your garden is 50% sand. If the silt layer is 1/4 inch deep, then 25% of the soil is silty, and the remaining 25% is clay.

Deductions can be made from your calculations and help you determine whether you're dealing with sandy soil, clay soil, or loamy soil.

The Hole Test

Although this test helps check for the texture and soil type, it also doubles as a way of determining soil drainage.

Dig a one-foot-deep by one-foot-wide hole somewhere in your garden.

Pour water into the hole and see how long it takes for all the water to drain out. Ideally, it should take anywhere from 10 to 30 minutes.

If the water drains completely in less than 30 minutes, then the soil is porous, and only drought-loving plants can grow in it. If it drains in three to four hours, then the drainage is poor. This shows there are large amounts of clay or minerals preventing water movement from the surface.

IMPROVING SOIL DRAINAGE

After finding out the soil type and drainage situation of your garden, you'll need to adjust and improve it if it does not suit your planting needs. Drainage problems can destroy your garden, obstruct plant roots from getting oxygen—leading to damage and disease infestation.

Fixing soil drainage can improve the situation of the garden. In many cases, high amounts of clay in the soil are the chief causes of minor garden drainage problems. This means that after heavy rainfall, there's standing water throughout the day. Since clay soil is dense and has tightly packed particles, rainwater does not filter easily. The clay soil will need improvement to fix these kinds of drainage issues.

The soil for planting needs to drain. Otherwise, it can cause significant issues for your plant health. The soil may eventually become compact and not allow water to penetrate, causing the leaching of nutrients. It can also cause the roots to suffocate and the soil to bake due to the lack of moisture to maintain soil temperature.

Here are some things to add to improve the drainage ability of dense soil (Mlgardener, 2021):

1. **Perlite**: Perlite is a lightweight volcanic rock with high water content. When exposed to heat, it pops like popcorn and expands. Adding perlite to the soil loosens it and stops clumping. The soil also gains water retention capacity, which boosts its quality.

2. **Sand**: Adding sand to a garden soil will break up the soil. The sand particles will permeate the soil lumps and scatter them. This improves drainage and allows the free flow of air into the soil.

3. **Compost**: The role of compost in fixing soil problems is underrated. Usually, dense soils do not have much organic matter. Organic matter in soils breaks up soil clumps to increase soil and plant nutrients. It soaks up water like perlite and helps maintain optimum soil conditions.

4. **Mulch**: Mulching is effective in increasing drainage. Although it does not work as fast as the others, the results are remarkable. Mulch retains water, and since it decomposes slowly, it prevents the soil from getting baked. Degrading insects and worms in the garden feed on it and

soften the soil in the process. The soil loosens
in two to four years of mulching.

5. **Vermiculite**: Just like perlite, vermiculite is a
glass-looking volcanic rock. It is highly
absorbent and can be combined with compost
or/and perlite to remedy hard soil. It breaks up
soils easily and improves plant health.

These procedures may not work too well for serious
garden drainage issues. A severe drainage issue means
that after a light to moderate rainfall, standing water
could last for a few days. Some of the reasons for this
kind of issue include high water tables, low grading
compared to the surrounding properties, hard materials sitting underneath the soil, etc.

Many garden owners choose to build an underground
drain, usually the French drain, as a remedy. To create a
French drain, make a ditch, fill it with gravel, and cover
it. People also use drainage wells to improve drainage
in highly compacted soils because it creates somewhere
for the water to run into when it rains.

Soil drainage can also be improved by building up the
soil in the affected location to redirect the flow of
water. However, making raised beds to stop drainage
problems in one area can cause drainage issues to
develop in another. To prevent this, the water should be

routed into the street or gutter if you can get permission for that.

Another popular solution is the creation of a rain garden or pond to collect extra rainwater. For gardens plagued with rainwater from neighboring buildings, fixing barrels to the downspouts to catch the rainwater that would normally clog the garden is a good idea. Also, the rainwater collected can later be used for watering.

You can also create a gravel channel. Dig a path for the water to be rerouted, but make it deeper and line it with pebbles and gravel. You can also bury pipes into the ground to divert the water to the location of your choice.

If the drainage problems in your garden cannot be fixed using any of the above means, get someone who is experienced to help you out.

SOIL PH

The pH of garden soil plays a vital role in the growth of plants. You must test the pH of your soil before planting because if the pH is not in the appropriate range, most plants will not access soil nutrients. When the pH of a soil is not within the optimal range for the plant, applying fertilizers or extra plant nutrients will be futile, as it will not yield any results. The pH of soil indicates how much hydrogen ions are present in the soil. The soil is acidic if the pH is less than 7, neutral at 7, and alkaline when it is higher than 7.

Having acidic or alkaline soil is not ultimately bad, as the plants you're growing will determine which pH level to settle for. The majority of plants prefer a soil pH of around 6–7.5. However, some plants prefer very acidic or alkaline soils (Iannotti, 2020).

The pH of the soil also determines nutrient availability, soil health, and the kind of plants you can grow.

Carrying Out a Soil pH Test

The best time to do a pH test on your soil is during fall. This gives you the chance to make adjustments before winter or spring. Doing the test in the fall also helps you identify the weeds that have grown in the soil during summer, which invariably leaves a clue about the soil pH. Acidic soil often favors dandelions, plantain, and wild strawberries, while an alkaline soil will allow the growth of Queen Anne's lace, chicory, and chickweed (Iannotti, 2020).

The Procedures for Doing a pH Test

Although there are test kits for testing soil pH, you can do the tests on your own in your garden without them.

All you need are various items for these different procedures.

Vinegar and Baking Soda Test (Iannotti, 2020):

- Scoop up 2 cups of soil from various areas of your garden. Get two containers
- , put a cup of soil in each container, and add water until the soil is muddy. Add a half cup of vinegar to the first container and stir lightly. If fizzing occurs, then your soil pH is alkaline
- (7-8). If the vinegar does not affect the soil, add a 1/2 cup of baking soda to the second container and stir lightly. If fizzing occurs when the baking soda is added, your soil pH is acidic
- (5-6). If there is no reaction from the vinegar or the baking soda, your soil pH is neutral at 7.

Red Cabbage Water pH Test (Helmenstine, 2020):

Fill a saucepan with two cups of distilled water. Slice around six red cabbage leaves into it. Let it boil for 10 minutes. Let it sit off the heat for 30 minutes. Drain out the liquid (purple or blue). The pH of this liquid is 7 (neutral).

Scoop two teaspoons of garden soil into a transparent container and add a few inches of cabbage water. Stir and observe after 20–30 minutes. The soil is acidic if the cabbage juice's color changes to reddish or pink. It is alkaline if the color changes to sea blue or yellow-green. If the color remains blue or purple, then the soil has a neutral pH.

Ensure that you're not using too much soil for the test. You'll have to redo the test if the juice changes to grayish black.

Using a Soil pH Test Kit

If you'd rather buy a pH test kit for your soil, that's okay too. The kits are affordable, simple, and effective. Although there are many different pH test kits on the market, the procedure for using them is almost the same.

One major difference, though, is that some kits are packaged with an already prepared pH test solution, but others include the test reagent in powder form for you to add distilled water.

The pH test kits are quite accurate for gardeners if adequate precaution is taken. Gardeners need to be careful during soil sample collection, prevent contamination, and monitor the time-lapse to get accurate readings.

You can get soil pH test kits in garden centers or online at Amazon.

Procedure for Using the Test Kit

After buying your test kit, follow these steps to do the soil pH test ("How To Use A Soil pH Test Kit," 2014):

- **Gather Your Equipment**: Use a clean trowel and container for your samples. If your test kit is powder-based, you have to get distilled water for the test.
- **Sample Collection**: Choose what part of your garden to get the samples. The pH of the soil in different parts of your garden varies. This could be natural or as a result of the levels of cultivation. If they're too distinct, you will notice the different colors, humus content, and texture.

Therefore, ensure you take samples from different areas and do separate tests for the samples. Also, don't forget to label.

Clear the top two inches of soil before you collect a sample from a spot. Doing this keeps your sample results free from interference by mulches or top dressings previously applied on the soil.

Dig to a depth of about five inches and scoop your sample from the bottom part. Collect more soil than you will need for your sample, so you have plenty left after removing stones, lumps, twigs, etc. Don't forget to label.

- **Sample Preparation**: Dry the sample after removing stones, lumps, and twigs. Use a dry trowel or teaspoon to mash the dry sample. Scoop the required amount of soil in the test tube or test container provided.

3

STEP 3- DETERMINE YOUR SUN AND WIND EXPOSURE

B esides soil and nutrients, the quality of your plants will also be affected by exposure to sun and wind. The amount of sunlight in your garden changes throughout the day with the movement of shadows. Some plants thrive in more than six hours of sunlight and are called full-sun plants. For some plants, however, their growth is better with less light. Before you start planting, check for the sunlight level of your garden.

Here's how to observe and understand the sunlight condition in your garden.

MONITOR THE SUNLIGHT

First, you have to know how much sunlight your garden and yard get on a daily basis. Track the light patterns at intervals during the day, making observations about the shadows and the length. Remember that trees without leaves may appear to have sunny spots underneath them in spring—however, summer and fall usher in heavy shade. Don't forget to take note of shadows from walls and buildings as you study the sun's path in your garden.

Get stakes or markers to note the light and dark areas in your garden. You can even create a lightmap on paper. Use some sheets of tracing paper to outline your garden.

Two hours after sunrise, start your recording. Find out the positions of light and shade and note them on the tracing paper—including the time.

Do this several times throughout the day on new sheets of paper. End the recording at about one hour before nightfall. Indicate the shady sections using a pencil. Ensure that your diagram indicates if the reflection is in the morning or afternoon. Combine all the sketches you've made to notice how your garden receives sunlight.

Don't forget to accurately label the sections of your garden where you take the sunlight measurements from, for instance, behind the oak tree, near the fence, etc.

If writing or making sketches will be tedious for you, use a camera or cell phone—Snap photos of your garden every hour to track the sunlight. While you do this, remember that the position of the sun changes at different intervals during the year.

The parts of your garden with sunlight almost all day (more than six hours) are direct to work with. With those kinds of spots, you're sure that the sun's intensity fluctuates at different times of the day.

The shady parts are harder to decipher. Some of the shaded regions are deeply out of the sun's reach and can only be suitable for plants that do not need direct sunlight.

Having deciduous trees in your garden provides seasonal shade. If there are leafless boughs, then try planting ephemeral plants underneath. Understand the seasonal light patterns of the existing plants (trees) in the garden as you choose a location for new plants.

Light Requirements Based on Region

Plants have different light requirements according to the part of the U.S. where they're native. The light requirements are not static. Some sun-tolerant plants in the south may require shade, while plants that love the sun may not get their full requirements due to the cloud covers if they're planted in the Pacific Northwest. Shade-loving plants can thrive in the hot sun of regions with cool, wet summers.

Plants and Light Requirements

While you use a sun map for your garden to figure out the extent of sun exposure, you need to know the different light requirements for plants. Most plants prefer full sun, part sun, full shade, or part shade. These terms describe how much sun they need for their optimum growth.

Full Sun

Full-sun plants require sunlight that shines right above them. Plants with this requirement need sunlight for more than six hours daily. Some can tolerate the sun from dawn to dusk. Plants with this label and heat or drought-tolerant capacity will grow well in summer no matter the sun's intensity. Plants having silver or gray foliage can also tolerate harsh amounts of sun.

However, even though some plants may be labeled "full sun," it is important to note their heat capacity. For instance, a plant labeled full-sun for the Appalachian mountains may have different lighting needs than full sun on the Gulf Coast. Cross-check all label recommendations for the plants you want, and let them guide you.

Part Sun and Part Shade

These terms are similar. Plants with the part-sun/part-shade requirement simply prefer to have between three to six hours of sun daily. These plants prefer dim light when they're not receiving direct sunlight in the morning or afternoon sun.

Part-shade plants are highly sensitive to extra sunlight and require shade when the sun is at its hottest.

Part-sun plants need more direct light than they need shade and may have poor growth if the sunlight is too little.

Full Shade

Full-shade plants can thrive on indirect light or deep shades. They usually do not need more than three hours of direct sunlight daily. If exposed to too much sun, shade plants can wilt. Planting these types of plants under other trees is excellent for their growth. The best kind of sun that is not sensitive to full-shade plants is the early morning or evening sun.

Reducing Shade in Your Garden

If the trees in your garden prevent you from having as much sunlight as your plants require, you can reduce the shade. Check for some of the trees that make dense shades with their branches and cut out the lower hanging branches. This act is known as "limbing up" and allows more sunlight into the leafy shade. If you have solid fences in your garden, try changing them to lattices to improve the light penetration.

Choosing Seeds to Match the Garden's Sun Exposure

When you map the sunlight exposure pattern of your garden, ensure the seeds you choose can suit the sun exposure.

When buying seeds, look at the seed packet to find out the sun requirements it needs.

Proper Row Orientation

When mapping sunlight for your garden, ensure to take note of fences, buildings, or trees that may be on or around your property. Before doing so, you probably know what plants you want to grow and whether they will shadow other plants. Most people prefer to plant their small crops on the southern part of their garden and larger plants around the north. For instance, if you're growing things like cabbage and sugar snap peas, it is better to plant the cabbage on the south of the sugar snap peas. Doing so will ensure that the cabbage plants do not have their sunlight obstructed by the sugar snap peas.

WIND EXPOSURE AND WIND-RESISTANT PLANTS

Exposure to sunlight isn't the only thing to worry about when you want to plant. There's something else: the wind.

Wind can affect the growth of plants, especially if the wind is strong enough to break the petals and stems of your plants. When plant stems are damaged, it results in a wound that leaves the plant susceptible to diseases.

Again, constant exposure to strong winds can make a plant container dry and stress the plant.

Stress in plants is detrimental to their growth. When there are regular strong winds, the leaves shut their pores to minimize the loss of water. Activating this causes slow growth to the plant because it reduces its ability to breathe. The ultimate result of this is low yield.

How to Prevent Bad Effects of Winds

- **Plant in Areas With Less Wind Interference:** This is the first thing to do. Check all the sites in your garden to determine the area with the most wind interference. If it's within your power, try planting in an area that gets the least amount of wind.

If physical observation is not enough to make accurate deductions, consult a reliable wind data source to know your location's average wind speed and direction.

- **Use a Strong Structure to Hold Weak Plants:** If you have tall plants, find a vertical rigid structure that you can tie them to, which will hold them up as they grow. The structure will also serve as a backbone and keep the stem from breaking.
- **Check Your Watering Pattern:** During the windy season, pay more attention to your plants and ensure they do not dry out fast. If they do, then water the plants more often to cushion the effect of the wind.
- **Select Low Height Species:** If your garden is in a windy place and you cannot plant in isolated spots, choose only plants with a low height.

Some plants are wind tolerant and will resist high winds.

- **Install Wind Buffers:** Besides attaching your plants to support structures, you can add physical barriers to buffer the wind. This stops physical damage to the plants. Ensure that a wind buffer is not built on the south side of the garden to prevent interference from the sun. Before you build a buffer, ensure you have carefully observed your garden so that you can choose the best spot with minimal wind interference and good sun exposure.

Continuous strong winds can make plants bend and shake from their roots. This makes the plants unable to stay firm in the soil. If they're not firmly rooted in the soil, the plant starts having trouble absorbing water and can even cause your plants to die.

Wind plays a huge role in plant growth and development. If the wind movement is too much, this causes poor growth and development. Plants that grow in windy areas often suffer from stunted growth.

Also, wind facilitates the spread of plant diseases from one location to another. Plants can become infected when the wind blows spores from disease-infested plants to healthy ones.

Using Plants for Wind Protection

If your garden is prone to excessive winds, you can protect it by using hardy trees and shrubs like American holly, cabbage palm, willow, etc.

These plants serve as windbreaks and protect the plants in your garden from the effects of harsh winds.

Wind-Resistant Plants for the Garden

Besides adopting windbreaks for your garden, you can go right ahead into planting wind-resistant plants.

Some plants are considered wind resistant because of the flexibility of their stems. They can tilt and sway without breakage or damage. Many of the plants with small narrow leaves have adapted to become wind tolerant.

While flowers are usually the first kind of plants to be affected by heavy winds, some flowers are wind tolerant and can do well in areas with harsh winds.

These are some hardy flowers that you can plant in your garden (Martin, 2020):

1. Gazanias: These are wind-resistant plants with bright flowers. Their full heir is 10 inches tall and around 10 inches wide.

They grow annually and do not need extra care. They are full-sun plants. Gazanias are in bloom from summer to fall.

2. Nasturtiums (*Tropaeolum majus*): They are famous for their wind tolerance. They can be planted directly in the garden after the last frost of the season.

3. Shasta Daisy (*Leucanthemum x superbum*): Shasta daisies are wind tolerant due to their sturdy stems and flowers. Shasta daisies produce lots of white flowers around the yellow center. Their average height is around three feet tall and up to two feet wide. Their sunlight preference is full sun, and they can grow in different kinds of soil. Aside from being wind resistant, they're also resistant to pests. Shasta daisies are perennials, although they don't live for very long.

4. Portulacas (*Portulaca grandiflora*): They are annuals that do not need extra care for their growth. They are both wind and drought resistant. Portulacas do not need frequent watering because the fleshy foliage maintains their moisture content. It always returns yearly due to its reseeding capacity.

5. Zinnia (*Zinnia elegans*): This is a rapidly growing wind-tolerant, long-term annual. The best variant is the low-growing species. Others have to be attached to stakes. The survival rate of a zinnia plant reduces drastically when you transplant them; therefore, do a direct planting in the garden during the warm spring weather.

6. Geraniums: They are wind-resistant plants great for window boxes and balconies. These flowers prefer lots of sunlight for their growth but require shade in hot summer afternoons. Geraniums are prone to fungal diseases, so only the plant's roots should be watered while the leaves remain dry. When the frost comes, geraniums have to be transferred indoors.

7. Marigolds (*Tagetes*): These annual plants produce colorful orange and yellow flowers in spring and summer. They require full exposure to sunlight for their growth. When the frost season is over, and spring is starting, you can plant marigold seeds.

8. Daylilies (*Hemerocallis spp.*): They are great wind-resistant flowers. These perennial plants grow colorful flowers that blossom and die off in one day. However, you can still get several blooms from the plant because a single stem produces over a dozen flowers. Daylilies need full sun for their optimum growth but require shade when the area is too hot.

9. Coreopsis (*Coreopsis spp.*): Coreopsis (tickseed) is both an annual and perennial plant. This wind-resistant plant is also great for garden pollination because it attracts insects and birds to its colorful flowers. The pink, yellow, white, or red flowers bloom in summer and occasionally in fall.

10. Azalea (*Rhododendron*): The *Rhododendron* is a perennial shrub that blooms colorful flowers. This plant grows optimally under partial shade and cannot withstand the hot afternoon sun. It has different colors like orange, pink, yellow, and white.

How to Landscape for Windbreaks

If you do not want to restrict your gardening or planting to hardy, wind-resistant flowers, you can plant windbreaks.

Windbreaks are rows of trees, shrubs, or fences planted to withstand and redirect wind. Windbreaks are common in farms to protect crops, buildings, or fields. However, you can use them in your garden to reduce the effect of wind as well as provide shade for flowers. Windbreaks have also been used to curb soil erosion and loss of moisture in gardens.

Here's how to create a windbreak in your garden:

1. Study the wind patterns in the garden to decipher the best location for a windbreak. Take height and width measurements of your garden and even get a sketch of it. Let this guide you as you choose the area for your windbreak.

2. Choose plants that already grow well around you; let the species be as local as possible. For extra recommendations, ask the local nursery or county extension service for suggestions on sturdy trees and shrubs with rapid growth. Consider the density and height of the windbreaks. You will get more wind reduction from taller windbreaks. Choose evergreen species like Cypress, Douglas, or Western Red Cedar. But if you want it to be more alluring, combine deciduous and evergreen shrubs or trees.

3. Clear the planting site to remove all unwanted vegetation. Do a soil test and make the appropriate adjustments.

4. Plant the windbreak perpendicular to the direction of the winds around 50–200 feet from the garden needing protection. Placing it beyond 50 feet increases the protection. Ensure the trees maintain a distance of two or three times their full height away from the home.

5. Ensure there is a distance of around seven feet between the trees to avoid overcrowding. Don't create too much gap between the trees or else, the effectiveness reduces. If the windbreak is thicker, plant two or more rows of trees, leaving 10 to 12 feet between them.

6. If using fruiting or flowering shrubs, plant them in front of tall trees to provide color and attract pollinators. Protect your garden with hardy shrubs like manzanitas, coyote brush, and ceanothus.

7. Start planting your windbreak plants in late fall to early spring so the roots become firm before the summer heat begins. Stick to the requirements of the plants used for windbreaks to ensure proper growth.

4

STEP 4- PLANNING AND PLANTING ACCORDING TO SPACE

E very beautiful and well-organized garden is the result of maintenance, money, effort, and time. Beginning your journey to flower gardening with a plan is the best way to reach better results faster and reduce the demand for resources. Before starting, devote some time thinking about the type of garden you want to have and how best to achieve it. You want to create a garden that accents your living space and continues to blossom for years to come.

Factors such as foot traffic routes, shade, drainage, sunlight, water, wind, and sunlight, must be taken into account. You also want to balance out the types of flowers you grow in your garden according to what you expect to get out of them. For your first step of planning and planting a garden, a landscape analysis is in order.

THE RIGHT PATH TO SPACING

Row planting is a common technique in gardening, but it comes at the cost of lesser yield. You stand to grow more flowers with no extra effort without it. In fact, the technique aims to create a walkway between plants for easier access. So it doesn't exactly fit if you're implementing row planting in a raised garden, for instance. Using a raised bed means that you want a compact growing area that allows you to reach your plants without the hassle of stepping into the growing area. This explains why raised beds tend to have fixed dimensions of less than or precisely four feet (GIM_Team, 2015).

These dimensions allow every type of gardener to access their plants easily. With the arm span of the average person capable of reaching two feet, it means that the midsection of the growing area can be reached from all sides. It'd be redundant to apply row planting methodology with such a clever growing technique. Instead, it would be best to consider planting by area (GIM_Team, 2015).

In this technique, you isolate a square area of your garden and split its breadth and length according to the plant's spacing needs. The labels on seed packets usually come with the recommended spacing and other measurements, so check before planting. The information will usually contain measurements for row spacing or seed spacing.

Since the goal is to maximize space and grow the most plants effectively, you should ignore the row spacing numbers. Instead, focus on the plant or seed spacing numbers, as it's important to divide your growing area by the number of seeds or plants being grown.

CREATING YOUR PLANTING SECTIONS

The go-to sectioning measurement is about a square foot. The measurement is a rough estimate because the thickness of the boards used for your beds will likely shrink the growing area to a little under one foot. But you have nothing to worry about: It's not like the plants would notice anyway. To make plant spacing more straightforward, it's common practice to use a spacing grid. You can make yours by measuring and cutting materials to fit the shape of your bed before securing the grid to the bed.

How Many Seeds Should You Plant per Section?

To set up your grid, you need to know how many seeds can be planted together and their spacing requirements. The process involves a bit of math to determine the accuracy and other parameters to ensure that everything is well laid out. Here is a step-by-step guide to determining the number of seeds or plants to go into a section (GIM_Team, 2015):

1. Identify the seed spacing information on the back of the seed or plant packet. For instance, you could use three-inch spaces per planted square foot.
2. Split the breadth of the growing area using the same measurement seed spacing (three-inch seed spacing). Say, for instance, the growing area is 12 inches in width. You'll have four sections across the bed using the three-inch seed spacing.
3. Repeat the second step across the length of the growing area, which will also be around 12 inches. Since the measurements are the same (length and breadth), you'll also have four longitudinal sections.
4. When you multiply or sum the number of square sections on your growing lot, you'll arrive at 16 spaces capable of housing a plant.

5. You're ready to plant at this point. With the three-inch plant or seed spacing, you can grow up to 16 plants at a time with one per square foot area of your growing lot.
6. Use the same steps for other growing areas of your garden for the same results.

CONSIDER FULL-GROWN PLANTS WHEN SPACING

The spacing of a landscape garden is the determining factor that tells it apart from a wild forest. Growing your flowers with too much space in-between can reduce the garden's beauty, making it look barren. The garden is well-dimensioned in both layout and spacing, inducing appeal and visual interest with the right design. The type of landscaping used, including the spacing applied to plants, differs from plant to plant. Bedding plants will typically require a different form of landscaping from shrubs or trees.

Annuals

Spacing between flowers doesn't matter as much for annual crops, as they often reach maturity within a planting year. Annuals can be planted a little closer together than most flowers since they mature faster. However, with the proper conditions, annuals will thrive better and blossom into significant clusters if planted with recommended spacing requirements.

Annual flowers usually come with guidelines for replanting and spacing. Ensure to follow the guide. Here are some common spacing details for some regular annual flowers (Ellis, 2021):

1. **Begonias:** Begonias' tubers can be planted 8 to 12 inches apart.
2. **Snapdragons:** Snapdragons should be planted between 6 to 10 inches away from each other.
3. **Cosmos:** Cosmos flowers grow better when spaced seven inches apart.
4. **Marigolds:** For best results, you want to plant smaller varieties of marigolds with an 8- to 10-inch spacing. Larger varieties can be spaced by up to 12 inches.

Perennials

Like annuals, perennial flowers will also have unique details on the healthiest ways to plant and space them. Since perennials last longer, proper spacing is crucial for lowering the risk of diseases due to lack of aeration and helping the plant's growth. At first, perennials may struggle to live up to their spacing. However, in due time, they will bloom and fill the space. Don't let the layout fool you into halving the space requirements, as you may work a double separating the plants when they bloom.

The standard guidelines for spacing perennials are as follows:

1. **Large Perennials:** 18 to 36 inches
2. **Medium-Sized Perennials:** 12 to 18 inches
3. **Small Perennials:** 6 to 12 inches

USE GRAPH PAPER TO MAP OUT THE GARDEN

Before you decide on the types of flowers to introduce into your garden or how to space them, you should have already figured out your planting areas. To begin, sketch a map of your growing lot. In your map, include existing flora like shrubs and trees and other details like patios, slopes, large stones, etc. Your map can be a formal graphical representation, complete with scales, or it could be casual and highlight crucial details. Whatever your choice, the goal is to ensure accuracy in your representations for better results. Take note of the types of flowers you wish to grow and how they factor into your plans.

Highlight areas that experience partial shade or full sunlight and indicate areas protected from wind or those with the best planting soil. Include access routes in your map(s). You don't want to plant a garden you will have to tiptoe around. The paths could be standard paths made of stones or bricks or frequently used areas. You also want to make some room to accommodate viewing angles. This will ensure that visitors to your garden can enjoy the view without ruining your plants.

Another vital detail that should not be missing from your map is sources of water. Whether you prefer an automatic irrigation system, traditional irrigation with watering cans, spigots, or underground sprinklers, your map should represent it, as well as details about how to proceed with it. Elevations are another defining factor that should be accounted for. Find out if your growing area rises toward the center or slopes toward the extremities. Understanding elevations help you with drainage. You'll want water to drain away from your home rather than toward it.

POPULAR PERENNIALS FOR SPACING REQUIREMENTS

Every flower garden is anchored on perennial plants, which, unlike annual plants that have to be harvested and replanted before and during spring, are left to die at the end of the season. However, they tend to regrow from their old roots during the start of new planting seasons. Perennials are preferred to annual crops because they require lower maintenance and can be relied on to perform well during the planting season. Additionally, they offer a variety of forms, colors, and textures to the garden.

Perennial flowers vary in form, culture, bloom period, and life span. Some types are known as the delphinium and lupines because they have the shortest life span of the lot, lasting for around three to four years. Other perennials have longer life spans, like peonies, which can live up to 15 years at a time. In terms of bloom time, while some perennials may bloom for a day, some bloom for a week or two, and others may be in bloom for more than two to three months at a time.

Here are some colorful, fragrant perennials to consider for your flower garden (Garrity, 2020):

1. *Dianthus*: *Dianthus* has multiple varieties that you can choose from, including the upright and creeping. Some have sweeter scents than others. This perennial comes complete with fringed petals, which may be any color ranging from peach to coral to white to pink. A *Dianthus* thrives best in sunny areas.

2. *Lavender:* Lavender is a popular perennial known for its scent and use in teas, scented items, and scones. You can harvest its dried buds to prepare any of these.

Lavender experiences a bloom period of several weeks during summer, depending on your variety.

3. *Asters:* As plants begin to lose their glow and color during the later periods of fall, asters come alive. They come in purple, pink, blue, or lavender. Every variety of this perennial thrives in sunlight and poliinators love it. Some types may be able to live through light frost.

4. *Chrysanthemums:* Chrysanthemums are another plant that blooms in the fall. They work as both annual and perennial flowers—depending on when you plant them. For a more perennial effect, try growing them between spring and midsummer. This way, their roots will develop properly, unlike in late fall, when they will still be unsettled and incapable of surviving the winter.

5. *Salvia*: *Salvia*, complete with spiky blooms, enjoys a good, full sun. As a result, they are more drought-tolerant when established and will bloom between mid to late summer for many weeks.

6. *Daylily:* If you struggle to grow plants on your growing lot, consider planting daylilies. They multiply each year and experience bloom time for one day—hence, their name. However, this perennial flowers well and enjoys a good dose of sunlight.

7. *Tradescantia*: Otherwise called the spiderwort, *Tradescantia* comes with beautiful bright flowers (purple in color) and grassy foliage. They are one of the easiest perennials to cultivate and can grow in any soil type. However, they enjoy moist soil with good drainage and lots of sun.

8. *Hellebore:* This beauty of a perennial can be added to your garden for some winter beauty. Hellebores are also known as Lenten roses because they experience bloom sometime around the period of Lent, between mid to late winter. This perennial grows best in shaded areas.

9. *Peony:* Peonies experience bloom time within late spring and early summer, with the plant growing bigger and better as the years go on. They enjoy lots of space and sun to grow and hate being moved, so avoid crowding when planting.

10. *Roman Chamomile*: This perennial is known for its scented flowers and the delicate tea that can be made from drying them out. Roman chamomile is good business for every flower lover and brings a certain vibrance to the garden. They're relatives to the German chamomile, which are annuals, and like a good dose of sunlight.

GROWING AND CARING FOR SEEDS AND BULBS

Bulbs refer to tiny pockets of flower power which take anywhere from a few weeks to months to yield results. However, they make up for the time by the eventual outcome. Bulbs are also used to describe other plants besides true bulbs, such as rhizomes, corms, tubers, and crops with tuberous root systems. Whatever the case, the same planting and planning details apply to every plant classified as a bulb. Bulbs are easily grown with little to no experience.

Types of Bulbs

Bulbs are typically classified into two main categories (Hagen, n.d.):

1. **Summer Bulbs:** This type of plant is otherwise known as tender bulbs and is usually grown in spring and typically bud leaves and flowers in the summer. Some common summer bulbs are elephant ears, caladiums, lilies, and gladiolus. While some of these plants experience bloom for extended periods, some only bloom toward the later part of summer. For instance, dahlias are usually still in bloom well into autumn. As the name connotes, summer bulbs prefer the

warmth of summer and have zero tolerance to the cold and frost of winter. They are best grown when the soil is warm and when frost is long gone. They can be bought ahead of the planting season and stored in a cool, dry place until ready for use.

2. **Spring Bulbs:** Otherwise known as hardy bulbs, spring bulbs are sowed during fall and spend the entirety of winter hiding out in the soil. During spring, they sprout and experience bloom.

Common spring bulbs are crocus, hyacinth, irises, allium, tulips, and daffodils. Spring bulbs are planted just before the onset of winter because only cold temperatures can disrupt their dormancy and help them bloom properly.

How to Buy Bulbs

Picking suitable bulbs is the first step to growing a healthy and lush garden. Here are some tips to consider (Hagen, n.d.):

1. When buying bulbs, feel them, make sure they're firm—not spongy or soft.
2. Bloom is only as good as the bulbs themselves, so take your time to select quality bulbs. Do

your homework and find out more about getting the perfect bulbs.

3. Seek out bulbs that aren't already growing out or sprouting roots. This goes for all types of bulbs—even lilies, which tend to have fleshy roots sometimes.

4. Go for bulbs with no signs of damage, mold, or disease. These are red flags to watch out for.

Timing for Planting Bulbs (Hagen, n.d.):

1. Zones 4 to 7: If your growing area falls into this range, consider planting your spring bulbs as soon as the ground grows cold. Check the soil temperature during evening hours and ensure an average of 40 °F to 50 °F before planting. Time your planting to fall between six to eight weeks before frost sets in and freezes the soil.

With proper planning, you can set your purchase period to fall around the planting time to save the bulbs from storage risks. Otherwise, store bulbs in a refrigerator until needed. For summer bulbs, you want to target between mid to late spring.

2. Zones 8 to 10: In zones that fall within this range, spring bulbs will have to be refrigerated for several weeks, say, up to 10 weeks. The freezing time varies according to the bulb you're planting. The refrigeration is to help prep the bulbs for when the soil becomes cool enough for planting. For summer bulbs, consider planting during the early to mid-periods of spring.

Here are the average planting periods for spring and summer bulbs and their respective zones (Hagen, n.d.):

Summer Bulbs

- Zones 8 to 19: Between late March and May
- Zones 4 to 7: Between May and June

Spring Bulbs

- Zone 10: Between late December and early January
- Zones 4 and 5: Between September and October
- Zones 6 and 7: Between October and a few periods of November
- Zones 8 and 9: Between November and early December

Identifying Ideal Locations for Growing Bulbs

Bulbs aren't very selective of where they can be planted. Given that the area is well-drained and experiences a good amount of sunlight (and sometimes shade), bulbs can be grown easily. Drainage is imperative to maintain the water level and prevent oversaturation, which may cause rotting. Sandy and loamy soil are the preferred soil types of growing bulbs because they have the best nutrient levels and drain well.

Bulbs that bloom early in spring can be grown under the shade of deciduous trees, allowing them to get adequate amounts of sunlight to bloom and shade as the plant grows. You should keep in mind that these plants will only bloom appropriately in such conditions during their first year. During the later parts of the season, they'll need lots of sunlight to store enough energy in their leaves for bloom the following year.

How to Grow Bulbs in Your Garden

Bulbs can be grown in layers. This technique involves digging the recommended depth for the bulbs, placing them into the hole, and covering it up with soil. Alternatively, the bulbs can be planted in individual holes. This technique is known as individual planting and is much easier to achieve using a bedding plant auger.

Here are the steps to growing bulbs (Hagen, n.d.):

1. Decide on the depth you want to plant your bulbs. Depth typically varies across bulbs, and the outcome differs, too. Lower depths mean late bloom—if the bulbs germinate, that is. On

the other hand, shallower depths put the bulbs at risk of damage by climatic conditions. If you can't identify the perfect depth for your bulbs, consider a depth of two to three times the height of your bulbs.

2. Prepare your growing lot by loosening the soil and working in organic materials to improve drainage and the soil's nutrient level. You can use special bulb fertilizers; stick to the directions on the packaging.

3. Plant the bulbs root-first with the pointy side facing up. If you can't identify the top and bottom of your bulbs, planting on its side is your safest alternative. This way, they'll germinate and work their way up.

4. Cover the planted bulbs with soil and sprinkle lightly with mulch. Water well to help the bulbs settle into place.

5. Consider protecting your bulbs from critters by installing chicken wire or wire mesh over your garden beds. Alternatively, you can grow them in wire cages or bulb baskets.

Harvesting Bulbs and Aftercare

After blooming, you can easily cut out the flower stem. This applies to all bulbs. Don't snip the foliage until they are yellow and begin to wilt by themselves. This process means that the leaves are generating and storing energy for the following growing season. Cutting the foliage early is bad business, as it may lead to poor performance of the bulbs in the next season. Sometimes, the plant may not recover.

1. **Summer Bulbs**: In warmer areas, summer bulbs can be left to sit in the soil. Cover with mulch during winter to prevent them from freezing over. In colder areas, dig them up and store them until the next planting season.
2. **Spring Bulbs**: In colder areas, spring bulbs can be left to sit in the soil. Sometimes, this helps them grow and multiply in the following plant season. For spring bulbs in warmer areas, choose ones that can be dug up, frozen, and stored against the pre-chilling period of the next planting season.

How to Dig Up Bulbs (Hagen, n.d.):

- Cut off any foliage and stems remaining above ground level on the bulbs.
- Carefully loosen the soil surrounding the bulbs and remove them gently. Be careful not to tug and break the roots.

- Shake gently to remove excess amounts of soil from the roots and bulbs.
- Spread out the bulbs on newspaper to dry in a cool and shady area. The drying period could last several days at a time. Ensure that the bulbs are beyond the reach of children and animals, as they can be poisonous if ingested.
- After drying, put the bulbs into a cardboard box with holes, a mesh bag, or an aerated paper. A bit of somewhat damp perlite or vermiculite will ensure that your bulbs aren't dried out before the subsequent use.
- Store the bulbs in a dry, dark, and cool place, with a temperature range of 50 °F to 60 °F.
- Regularly evaluate your bulbs for signs of decay, rot, or mold. It could be weekly, biweekly, or monthly.

Tips for Growing Bulbs

1. Bulbs have to breathe every now and then, hence the use of mesh bags, perforated boxes, and aerated paper. Avoid using plastic or airtight containers to store your bulbs.
2. Avoid storing or pre-chilling bulbs in the same refrigerator as vegetables and fruits, particularly apples. This is because fruits and

vegetables give off ethylene gas, which is harmful to the plants contained in the bulbs.

3. If you must leave your bulbs in the soil during dormancy periods, ensure to leave markers to pinpoint their location after trimming the foliage.

4. You want to grow your bulbs within the planting season you bought them in.

5. For vibrant colors during bloom, consider planting your bulbs in soil with a pH of 6 or 7.

ANNUALS

Growing annual flowers in pots or beds kicks off a yearlong parade of vibrant, beautiful leaves and flowers in your garden. For annuals, it's a different race throughout the growing season, as they have to unfurl their flowers and display their eye-catching foliage well until frost sets in. Due to their relatively shorter life span, it's important to know how to plant them and quickly start the season. To pull it off successfully, you must understand how annual flowers tick. While some annuals love the warmth and sizzle of summer, others fancy the cooler periods of a growing season to show their flair.

Usually, garden centers and seed markets sell annuals as the season arrives or is at hand. If you are unsure, you can always ask questions for clarity. Knowing your way around the suitable annuals to buy for each season is particularly important during the early periods of spring, just as summer annuals begin to grow within the cozy walls of greenhouses. Once they leave that habitat for the cold nights of spring, some may cease growing altogether. This is true for annuals that prefer heat, as early planting may mean the death of the plant due to cool soil and chilly air. This can often cause rot and may stall plant growth.

The ideal planting period for these annuals are cloudy days, as overcast skies shield the seedlings from sun stress just as they settle in with their new habitat. Alternatively, you can plant them in the evening just as the sun clears from the sky. This technique allows the plants to recover and settle in snugly before the sun comes up.

However, if you have settled on a sunny day, erecting a shading device would be critical to the survival of your seedlings. A bedding plant or cardboard propped up to lend its shade does the job. Before sowing your annuals into a garden bed, it's best to arrange the plants in pots in the order that they will appear in the beds. Customize the spacing using the size of mature plants. Allowing your annuals enough room to spread facilitates growth.

Planting annuals isn't hard and can be managed with the right know-how. Before removing them from pots or cell packs, consider watering the plants. During planting, ensure that root balls are moist to improve germination.

When transplanting, avoid tugging at the plants to prevent breaking. Instead, gently squeeze around the pot before flipping it over. Keep a hand on the stem and gently ease the plant out of the container. Next, you want to dig up a shallow hole with a trowel or your hand. The size of the hole depends on the size of the root ball. When planting annuals, it may benefit you to apply the stab-and-plant technique used by landscapers.

To do this, handle the trowel with the concave side tilted up and the blade facing down. Jam the trowel into the soil and push the handle forward. This should leave a hole behind the blade. Put the annual into the hole and cover the plant with soil.

The stab-and-plant technique is best used for loose soil types. After planting, always water your annuals with a hose-end sprayer, watering can, or watering wand, which bathes the plant in gentle showers. Ensure that the soil is thoroughly soaked and sprayed with mulch to reduce evaporation, lock in moisture, and prevent the growth of weeds.

5

STEP 5- FEEDING YOUR GARDEN

COMPOSTING

Compost refers to organic materials used to improve the soil's nutrient level. Currently, about 30 percent of the world's waste is made up of yard waste and food scraps, both of which could be composted for food production. By composting, these materials don't make it to landfills, where they would only decompose and create greenhouse gases which would further harm the environment ("Composting At Home," 2021).

Compost is typically made of three main ingredients:

- **Water:** The right volume of water is crucial for the development process of compost.

- **Greens:** This could be materials ranging from coffee grounds to vegetable waste, grass clippings, and fruits scraps, among others.
- **Browns:** These materials are already decaying matter like twigs, branches, and dead leaves.

When making compost, your pile should contain equal measures of greens and browns. Additionally, ensure your organic matter is of varying sizes to ensure better mixing and breaking down. While the greens provide the compost with nitrogen, the browns infuse carbon into the process, and water adds moisture to facilitate the decomposition of the organic matter ("Composting At Home," 2021).

Things That Can and Cannot Be Composted

Compost is meant to enrich the growth of plants. However, if done wrong, it can lead to stunted growth or death of the plants. Worst-case scenarios, they could potentially harm the consumers of the plants; therefore, it is vital to know the difference between materials that can and cannot be composted.

Allowable compost materials:

This includes leaves, paper, tea bags, eggshells, vegetables, fruits, straw, houseplants, hay, yard trimmings, cardboard, rags (wool and cotton only), fur, hair, fireplace ashes, sawdust, grass clippings, shredded newspaper, coffee filters (as well as grounds), and nutshells ("Composting At Home," 2021).

Disallowed compost materials ("Composting At Home," 2021):

- Eggs and dairy products like yogurt, sour cream, and butter cause odor problems that attract rodents and pests like flies.
- Fish or meat scraps and bones are not good for compost because they attract flies and rodents and produce foul odors during decomposition.
- Yard trimmings from chemically treated plants are unhealthy because they introduce chemicals into the compost, which may harm good microbes.
- Charcoal or coal ash, avoid these as they contain chemicals that are harmful to plants.
- Plants with insects or diseases. This goes without saying, as the insects and diseases are more likely to stick to the compost and transfer to new plants.
- Pet wastes like soiled cat litter or cat or dog feces are dicey, as they may contain pathogens, bacteria, parasites, germs, or viruses that are detrimental to health.
- Oils, lard, grease, and fats are harmful for the

same reasons as fish and meat additions. They develop odors and attract pests and rodents.
- Black walnut tree twigs and leaves should be avoided, as they give off chemicals that may harm plants.

If you are unsure about other things to add to your compost, consider paying your local recycling or composting office a visit. It will also help you know the materials allowed in composts in your locale.

Making Your Own Compost

There isn't a one-size-fits-all approach for composting. You can use a variety of methods and arrive at the same result. Here, we'll cover one of the basic forms of composting. For this process, you'll need tools like water hoses with spray heads, machetes, square-point shovels, and pitchforks. Ensure to mix the compost regularly and drizzle with water from time to time to help maintain the compost and speed up the process.

Here are some composting methods to consider ("Composting At Home," 2021):

Indoor Composting

This composting method is for when you can't set up an outdoor compost pile. Compost can be made indoors with a specialized bin, which you can find at your local gardening supplies store or hardware store. Alternatively, you could just make one yourself. Whatever the case, ensure to regularly maintain your compost and be mindful of what you add to the pile. Compost will not produce odors or attract pests and rodents if appropriately maintained. Your compost may be ready for use within two to five weeks, depending on the volume and materials used.

Backyard Composting

Pick a dry area of your yard with a shady spot and water source, and place your compost bin or pile there. Add your greens and browns as they come, ensuring to shred or chop up larger pieces. Drizzle with water as you add dry materials. Allow decomposing until the pile is established. Then, add green waste and grass clippings, and mix thoroughly. Add vegetable and fruit wastes—burying them about 10 inches beneath the compost pile. Feel free to cover the compost bin or pile with a tarp to help lock in moisture. Your compost is ready when it achieves a rich, dark color. It can take between two months to two years to accomplish this.

Why Should You Compost?

1. Compost costs little to nothing to make. All you need is kitchen waste, leaves, vegetation, and lawn clippings you'd otherwise pay to have

taken away. If anything, you're saving on waste disposal.

2. With compost, your plants will do well without fertilizers because compost is made up of the major nutrients required by plants, such as potassium, phosphorus, and nitrogen. Compost also provides other vital micronutrients, including zinc, iron, boron, copper, manganese, cobalt, molybdenum, and iodine.

3. Compost boosts the fertility level of the soil and helps plants develop healthy root systems by improving aeration levels of the soil and soil texture and structure. The organic matter used in compost feeds microorganisms, managing soil health and maintaining soil balance.

4. Soils and potting mixed with compost result in vibrant plants regardless of the crops grown in them: flowers, vegetables, herbs, etc.

5. Compost helps improve water retention in sandy soils and loosens clay soils.

6. Keeping trash out of landfill sites and recycling them for use in planting helps the environment become safer for everyone.

Composting Tips

Here are some tips for converting your wastes into compost without any stress (Vinje, 2013):

- Before adding new materials to your compost bin or pile, shred them into tiny bits. Smaller materials mean faster decomposition and better mixing.
- Instead of adding bits of new materials every now and then, collect new additions until substantial before introducing them into the compost bin or pile. This will improve heat levels and speed up decomposition.
- Use a compost crock or pail to store food scraps or wares until they are suitable enough to be added. This should save you frequent visits to the compost bin.
- Consider starting new compost with cottonseed meal, compost starter, blood meal, or well-aged manure. Not only are they richer in nitrogen, but they also help induce heat, which triggers microbes to decompose organic matter into compost.
- Turn your compost regularly. This will help with aeration, providing oxygen to the microbes and speeding up the process.

- Avoid using plants or organic matter containing herbicides or pesticides.
- Consider using activators to speed up the composting process or store your bin or pile in the sun, as microbes perform faster in warmer conditions.
- Finished compost can be introduced into the garden around two to four weeks before the planting season. This allows the compost time to settle into and enrich the soil.
- Check your compost before applying. When ready, it should have the look of rich, dark soil, as well as the right smell and texture. If the items you composted still appear visible, then it's not ready. Another marker to watch out for is volume and density. Finished compost is denser but half the size of the prior materials.

IRRIGATION

As you gear up to plant your flowers, you also have to consider how to get water to them, especially in warmer seasons when water loss occurs easily. There are various ways to irrigate your garden, each with its unique pros and cons. During irrigation, the configuration, location, and size of your growing area are key factors that determine a system that would best suit your garden.

Types of Irrigation System

Deciding on the correct irrigation system to use in your garden helps conserve water while regularly supplying adequate amounts to the plants. With an irrigation system, you can control how much water is allowed into the garden at any one time. This control makes irrigation systems better than manual watering with a can or garden hose. Besides hand watering, there are other ways to irrigate your garden, each with its unique pros and cons.

Soaker Hoses

Soaker hoses don't seem any different from regular garden hoses, except they are made of porous materials from which water seeps into the garden. When laid across the surface of your garden, water hoses will provide your plants with a steady water supply. For the most part, soaker hoses are built using polyethylene plastic and rubber, although some tend to be made from polyurethane and are BPA-free.

Pros

- Soaker hoses are a cheap investment for your flower garden because they are often hooked up to timers to save water, reducing your water bill. Soaker hoses water the crops intermittently.

- They provide reliable water availability for the garden at ground level, watering the soil instead of foliage and preventing the risk of fungal growth.
- Soaker hoses seldom clog, which makes them an ideal investment.
- With soaker hoses, you don't necessarily need a pressure regulator. Water pressure can be managed by closing and opening the water source.
- The installment of a soaker hose is simple. The process is as straightforward as hooking it up to a rain barrel or faucet and placing it near your plants.

Cons

- The best of soaker hoses can be seen in gardens with level grounds as pressure adjustment differs along the length of the hose.
- Soaker hoses aren't the most versatile irrigation system out there in terms of configuration potentials. For instance, you can shut off

certain parts of a soaker hose and leave other parts open.

- When a soaker hose goes bad, the repair is challenging, if not impossible. Damages like wear and tear and sun degradation are a given with repeated use. However, the severity of the damage can be managed by sprinkling a light layer of mulch over the hose.
- Soaker hoses have less precision in comparison to other forms of irrigation and cannot be operated underground.
- Soaker hoses also have a poor radius of coverage, meaning you'd need extra-long ones or several at a time to cover a larger garden.

Sprinkler Irrigation

Sprinkler irrigation systems are one of the more effective types of irrigation, especially for large gardens. This approach uses less water than some other forms of irrigation, although they are often prey to evaporation and lose a good amount of their water volume this way. Also, since sprinklers have a better coverage radius, they may aid weed growth in the garden, particularly in areas lacking mulch. The design also plays a part in the efficiency and effectiveness of a sprinkler system. The best designs are often those with a grid design that contain multiple sprinkler heads and cover the entire garden.

If installed incorrectly, sprinkler systems will likely water the foliage of plants, putting them at risk of foliar diseases. To prevent this, consider watering the plants during the early morning hours or the late evening hours. This way, the spread of diseases would be limited, and the loss of water to evaporation will be significantly less.

Pros

- Sprinkler systems have better efficiency in gardens with medium to coarse soil texture.
- Water volume can be controlled and applied at low rates.
- Sprinkler systems allow the use of chemigation and fertigation. The irrigation water can be injected with chemicals to control pests and improve plant nutrition.
- The center pivot system of sprinklers can be automated to begin and end at your desired time or area.

Cons

- Sprinklers may need to be used repeatedly to improve areas plagued by soil depletion.
- Since the area of coverage includes foliage, plants may suffer scalding.
- Center pivot tires may lead to deep ruts in gardens with clay soil.
- Poor-quality water can lead to clogging in the nozzles of sprinkler systems.

Furrow Irrigation

This irrigation system involves the use of several ditches to move water across the garden. Furrow irrigation is backbreaking work and has to be set up as soon as the crops are planted. Furrow irrigation systems favor gardens planted as rows of raised beds that are six inches in width and five to six inches in height.

Around 30 to 38 inches of space should be between raised beds to allow the creation of furrows for irrigation. That said, the furrows are linked to a ditch at one end of the garden, which runs down to the furrows placed between the garden beds. When water is introduced into the ditch, it flows into the furrows, which waters the garden beds ("Irrigation methods," n.d.).

Pros

- Equipment needed for furrow irrigation systems is relatively cheap.
- You can easily recycle runoff water for better efficiency.
- It conserves water better than cascading the garden would.

Cons

- The garden has to be graded to allow for equal distribution of water.
- It's one of the least effective irrigation systems, as water is subject to running off, infiltration, and evaporation.
- Installing and removing levees takes significant time and effort.

Drip Irrigation

Drip irrigation systems are made up of long tubes containing emitters. Secondary tubes are attached and directed away from the main water line, which is usually connected to a source, like a tap, and fitted with backflow valves, filters, and pressure regulators. Drip systems are made using polyethylene plastic and can be found at your local hardware store or an irrigation supply store.

Drip irrigation typically comes in two forms, namely:

1. **Drip Tape:** This type of drip irrigation uses flat-style tubes, which must be fitted with pressure reducers to work correctly. Drip tapes work best for subsurface applications, although they are designed to last only a handful of seasons at best.

2. **Drip Line:** This type of drip irrigation system is made using heavy-duty plastic and is designed to outlast drip tapes. Drip lines can be obtained with already-installed emitters—this type is better for when you want to plant intermittently. Drip lines with separate emitters are best for when you want to customize the spacing, in which case you'll have to fit the emitters yourself.

Pros

- Drip systems consist of multiple parts which are easy to install. Drip systems can be customized to reach some areas of your garden while limiting or inhibiting flow to other areas. This means you can choose the amount of water that reaches any part of the garden at any one time, making drip irrigation the suitable system for large gardens. This is especially so when there are areas left to fallow late or early during the planting season.

- Drip irrigation systems are designed to water the base area of plants, leaving little to no chance for evaporation or misdirection.

- Drip systems function properly with timers and can be used with automated scheduling. For instance, you can program it to water the garden at night in summer when evaporation wouldn't be a risk.

- In the event of damages, drip systems can be easily repaired and reconfigured with replacement parts. The process typically involves fixing and splicing, which can be done without special tools or skills.

- For gardens planted on slopes, pressure emitters can be fitted to compensate for the imbalance and ensure equal amounts of water for all areas of the garden regardless of their place on the slope. Additionally, you can get customized emitters that suit the type of soil in your garden.

Cons

- Drip systems require a significant up-front investment to set up. They also need to be carefully planned and can be a time-consuming venture.
- In some areas, the direction of drip irrigation can be misdirected by wind, resulting in water wastage or irrigation of the wrong areas of the garden. To avoid this, do not start up the system during strong winds and ensure that the drip line is parallel to the ground. You also want to ensure that the system "drips" instead of sprays.
- Clogging is a potential occurrence in drip system emitters. Hence, you'd have to do routine maintenance and conduct regular periodic inspections.

Subirrigation

Subirrigation is an irrigation system that provides crops with water just beneath the soil's surface. The system involves ditches and pipes and improves and manages water tables to the desired depth. Subirrigation systems usually involve permanent installations below the roots of plants.

Pros

- It requires the least effort of the other forms of irrigation.
- It can also be used as a drainage system for excess water.
- It helps to reduce water loss from evaporation.
- It's suitable for soils with poor water retention.

Cons

- Subirrigation only works well in gardens with level and smooth topographies.
- For optimum performance, the soil must be permeable and uniform.
- The system demands adequate water to run well across a growing season.
- Water containing high salt content doesn't work well with subirrigation systems.

Flood Irrigation

Flood irrigation waters a growing area using ditches or pipes. In this system, water can glide across the soil and between the crops. Gates and levees are used to manage the depth and volume of the water. For instance, flood irrigation systems are staples of rice fields in Missouri, which apply the side-let or cascade approach ("Irrigation methods," n.d.). In the former, layflat pipes are set up next to the levees. Next, the pipes are perforated to provide water to every area of the growing lot. For the latter, water is poured into the growing area from the highest point of elevation and is allowed to flow through various levee gates.

Pros

- The cost of procuring equipment is usually low.
- Runoff water can be recaptured and reused with better efficiency.
- The cascade approach wastes 60% more water than the side-inlet flood method.

Cons

- Flood irrigation has the poorest efficiency of the other irrigation systems. It has the highest water loss rate due to runoff, infiltration, and evaporation.
- The process of setting up and removing levees involves lots of time and effort.
- The land has to be graded to ensure uniform water distribution along the surface.

Which Irrigation System Is Best?

Knowing the ideal irrigation system to use puts your plants at an advantage and helps to lower the risk of self-inflicted errors.

When to Use Subirrigation

Subirrigation isn't the most common form of irrigation in semi-arid or arid regions where irrigation is a necessity for the germination of crops. Often, it is used as a part of a system of controlled and subsurface drainage.

When to Use Drip Irrigation

Drip irrigation is arguably the most effective form of irrigation. It is well suited to large gardens with a grid system of long and straight rows. The versatility of this system makes it ideal even for areas with slopes. Although the initial cost can be high, the system doesn't stop giving for years, making it rather practical for the price.

When to Use Soaker Hoses

Soaker hoses are best used in smaller gardens with level surfaces. For the most part, they are pretty inexpensive to acquire and have a relatively straightforward installation and configuration process. All you need to do is place it around your plants. They are excellent for raised beds.

When to Use Flood Irrigation

Although flood irrigation was primarily used in agricultural irrigation, its best use is in residential landscaping. It is especially common in regions with high water availability, where a system is needed for managing flooding and other related issues.

When to Use Sprinkler Irrigation

Sprinkler systems work best with tree, field, and row crops, as they can project water below or beneath the foliage. Sandy soils thrive with sprinklers due to the high infiltration rate, although sprinklers can also work on other soils. The key feature of this irrigation system is its adaptability to slopes, be it undulating or uniform.

When to Use Furrow Irrigation

This irrigation system works for a wide range of crops, especially ones suited to row planting. Furrows are your go-to if you have crops that may suffer damage from watering their crowns or stems. It also works well for watering tree crops.

Irrigation Tips (Thompson, n.d.):

- **Regular Inspection and Cleaning of Filters:** If your irrigation system uses filters, like drip irrigation, for instance, regular inspection and maintenance are compulsory to maintain the system's efficiency. Filters are crucial elements of these systems and help keep dirt and debris from clogging up the system and jamming the tiny openings in emitters. Routinely inspecting and cleaning out the screens in filters will leave your system running efficiently, which, in turn, guarantees healthy plants.

- **Deep Watering Over Frequent Watering:** You want to go for slow, deep irrigation when watering your crops. Applying water too quickly can result in runoff, which is wasting water. On the contrary, slow watering ensures that water seeps deeper into the soil. Drip irrigation shines in this aspect, although sprinklers can also do the job once the water flow is reduced. Run your irrigation system long enough for the water to seep at least six inches into the soil. The deeper the irrigation, the healthier the roots of your plants.

Shallow and frequent watering will erode the soil's surface, thus exposing the roots to risks like drought. However, operating at a reduced frequency will allow the soil some time to dry between irrigation. As your plants grow, you can adjust the irrigation system to match their needs. Since mature plants have a deeper and more extensive root system, irrigation should be deeper and less frequent.

- **Identify the Soil in Your Growing Area:**
  Before deciding on the type of irrigation system you want, determine your soil type, as it is an essential factor in the water's penetration rate and how much water reaches the root level of your plants. Soil types are divided into three: sand, loam, and clay. Clay soils have a denser structure with tightly packed particles, which means slower water penetration to the roots of plants. Instead, water is accumulated on the surface, closer to the shoots and foliage, but never fully reaching the roots.

Sandy soil has the fastest water penetration rate due to its larger and loosely packed particles. Loamy soil is the most balanced soil type, with good water penetration and retention. Plants growing in clay soil will benefit from slow drip emitters, but this same system will fail to grow plants sown in sandy soils.

- **Perform Regular Maintenance on Your Irrigation Systems and Sprinklers:** A leaky tap may not seem like much, but if left unchecked, it can flood your house. The same logic applies to irrigation systems. Broken or dysfunctional sprinkler heads or leaky taps and faucets will result in a considerable loss of water. Periodic evaluation of your equipment and irrigation systems can help you manage how much you spend on water and maintenance. Check for jams in sprinkler heads, as well as burying, breaks, dysfunctions, and leaks too. Hoses connected to taps and emitters can also have leaks and should be checked.

- **Mulching:** Apart from improving the look of your garden, mulching is a crucial technique in modern agriculture, with a diversity of uses ranging from managing soil erosion to preventing the growth of weeds. In terms of water management, mulching can help decrease evaporation and is excellent for locking in moisture within the soil. Mulches come in different forms, like plant-based, pine-straw, and wood. Whatever the type you use, they introduce organic matter into the soil over time, which boosts water retention in your garden.

- **Automate With Smart Tech:** You might want to consider upgrading your irrigation system to have automated controllers and/or rain sensors. Smart weather controllers evaluate the moisture of the soil and the weather to schedule watering of the garden using the data collected from the landscape. Rain sensors aren't expensive, and with some retrofitting, they can work with a wide range of irrigation systems. With that said, you want to adjust your irrigation to be in line with present conditions. The needs of your plants will change over the planting season, so ensure that you make the appropriate adjustments to accommodate your plants.

Regardless of your level of tech-savviness, automating your irrigation is an easy way to save on utility bills and landscape maintenance while protecting your crops and maximizing the efficiency of your irrigation system.

- **Manage Water Runoff:** Heavy application of water in the garden leads to runoff, regardless of how the water is applied—either by irrigation systems or natural rainfall. In residential landscaping, runoff implies water overflow over impervious surfaces like sideways and driveways, among others. Runoff is harmful to your garden for many reasons, like how it pollutes natural waterways, wastes water, and erodes soil particles and chemicals (e.g., pesticides, herbicides, etc.) into bodies of water. Managing runoff ensures water conservation within the garden, where it is most helpful to plants.

Here are some tips for managing runoff:

1. Align your downspouts to lead into the garden instead of outside into the streets or other areas.
2. Slow irrigation helps to reduce runoff. Think of drip irrigation and soaker hoses, which deliver low volumes of water at once.
3. Use mulch on hard surfaces such as concrete walkways to ensure water infiltration.
4. Ensure your sprinkler heads don't directly irrigate driveways, sidewalks, and roads.
5. Rain gardens can be used to capture water in sloped areas. You can also use downspouts to conserve rainwater.

FERTILIZING

Among the many things needed for healthy growth and vibrant blossoms, like sunlight and water, flowering plants require fertilizers. Potassium, phosphorus, and nitrogen are three essential nutrients necessary for plants to achieve their highest quality. Potassium and phosphorus help produce flowers and grow and develop the root system, while nitrogen is responsible for the healthy development of vibrant stems and leaves. Usually, gardeners use various fertilizers to feed their plants, although desired results can be obtained with all-purpose plant fertilizers.

As a rule of thumb, apply fertilizers just before your plants begin flowering or experience rapid growth. Granular fertilizers work best for preparing flower beds in fall or spring, while liquid fertilizers should be used immediately after planting. Expert flower gardeners advise using balanced fertilizers, which contain equal measures of potassium, nitrogen, and phosphorus. A good example is the 10-10-10 blend. This balance is necessary because fertilizers with unequal percentages will affect the plants differently. For instance, fertilizers with higher nitrogen content will produce vibrant leaves, but the production of flowers will be lower.

Types of Fertilizers

Since fertilizers are chemicals, they can be of both natural and synthetic makes. The application also differs, as some can be applied directly to the soil, and others may be applied to seeds in the form of coatings just before planting is done.

1. **Organic Fertilizers:** As the name connotes, organic fertilizers come from natural, biodegradable materials. They are generally eco-friendly and may contain any or all of the following elements: animal manure, peat moss, seaweed, mineral deposits, and compost. Organic fertilizers are one of the more versatile types, as they work well in both gardens and fields. Once applied, they immediately begin infusing the soil with beneficial nutrients that improve plant growth. Additionally, they increase the productivity and health of soil over time.

2. **Chemical Nitrogenous Fertilizer:** This fertilizer has high nitrogen content. However, this nitrogen transforms into ammonia, which dissolves into the soil after application when water from the irrigation system or rainfall saturates the garden. Once dissolved, the fertilizer's nutrients seep into the soil and travel toward the root systems of plants. Usually, nitrogenous fertilizers come in pellets or as white granules. They are typically applied during or before planting.

3. **Biofertilizer:** Naturally, many important microorganisms are crucial to the growth and development of plants. These microbes help break down nutrients for easier absorption by plants. The use of these microorganisms can be further improved by human intervention by selecting and evaluating organisms with the most efficiency. After, the organisms are cultured and applied to the soil via direct application or as coatings for seeds. The application of the cultured microbes may also be done using carrier materials and are regarded as biofertilizers.

4. **Inorganic Fertilizers:** Inorganic fertilizers have no definite form. They can be granular, powdered, or liquid, and as such, they will require different forms of application. For the most part, inorganic fertilizers are made up of concentrated ammonia that has been diluted with water. They are usually used to treat industrial fields, as they are the least expensive of the lot and can undergo synthesis with less effort than other fertilizer types. In comparison to organic fertilizers, the inorganic types are less bulky, meaning plants can easily absorb nutrients.

5. **Complete Fertilizer:** Compound fertilizers are

hardly ever made to suit several soil types at once. Hence, fertilizers that are made up of over two elements or minerals in reasonable ratios are better suited. Such fertilizers are made to suit the different soil types they are applied to. A mixture of several fertilizers reduces many deficiencies in soils and plants. In addition, these fertilizers aren't labor-intensive, and a typical blend would consist of primary plant nutrients like potassium, phosphorus, and nitrogen. Such fertilizers are known as complete fertilizers.

Forms of Fertilizers

Fertilizers can take various forms ranging from granular to liquid to powder. Granular fertilizers are easy to apply and sit on top of your soil. As you water the garden or rainfall occurs, the nutrients in the granules will be diluted and washed into the soil over time. Powdered fertilizers require water before application. Although you can spread them by hand, they also need watering to fully absorb into the soil. Liquid fertilizers are diluted with water before use. The application process is similar to watering your garden and can be done using a hose.

Tips for When and How to Apply Fertilizers to Your Garden

1. For annuals, you want to add your fertilizer when preparing the flower beds. The second application should come between six and eight weeks after. If your annuals will still experience bloom well into fall, a third application may be in order toward the later parts of August and should be at the same rate as the first two.

2. When applying fertilizers to new flower beds, work the fertilizer into the soil about four to six inches deep before planting. When planting established crops, you want to spread the fertilizers around the plants. Use a rake to carefully work it into the soil before watering thoroughly to allow the fertilizers to settle. If you can, pull apart the layers of mulch surrounding the crops to apply the fertilizers directly to the soil. This way, the mulch will lock in the nutrients as well and prevent runoff.

3. Use the recommended amount of fertilizer based on the type of plants you're growing, and take into account your soil test report for each period of the growing season. Understand that factors such as soil type, fertilizer type, plant health, and weather conditions, among others,

tend to influence the nutritional needs of plants as well as the timing of fertilizer application.

4. For established perennials and ornamental crops, fertilizers should be applied as growth continues during spring. A second application may be in order for perennials that experience longer bloom or longer-lasting foliage. The application rate should be the same as the first and can come six to eight weeks later.

5. Fertilizers should be applied to the flower beds of new ornamental crops and perennials during preparation. A second application should ensue after six to eight weeks.

6. Summer bulbs can be fertilized when growth restarts in spring. Plants with shorter bloom periods should get a second dose of fertilizer after flowering. On the other hand, those with extended boom periods, like dahlias and cannas, can receive a second application at a similar rate sometime in mid-July.

7. Wildflowers tend to have lower nutrient requirements than most plants. As a result, fertilizer should be applied once during spring, just as new growth shows. Alternatively, you can apply your fertilizer when preparing the garden beds.

8. Roses require separate fertilizer applications

around May, June, or July. Ensure that fertilization is satisfactory on or before the middle of July, as it'd only encourage new growth that may not fully acclimatize or harden enough during fall to survive the chill and frost of winter.

9. Spring bulbs should be fertilized once new growth emerges in spring. Time your second application of fertilizer to fall during the preparation of beds at some point in the later and early periods of August and September.

6

STEP 6- PROTECTING YOUR GARDEN

DISEASES

P lant diseases refer to crops' impairments, which disrupt or alter their normal, vital functions. All plant species, both cultivated and wild, can contract diseases. However, every species has its own unique diseases, usually few in number. How many diseases and when they occur in plants differ from season to season, depending on the type of crops and varieties planted, environmental conditions, and pathogens. While no plant is entirely immune to diseases, some experience more in their life cycles than others, which have better disease resistance.

Up to 85% of all plant diseases can be traced to fungal or related organisms, although bacterial and viral organisms can cause severe diseases in crops. Another causal factor is some nematodes. Plant diseases can also be classified as abiotic, caused by growth in problematic conditions, air pollution, toxicity, and nutritional deficiency. Such conditions are mostly noninfectious (Isleib, 2012).

Sources of Plant Diseases

The movement of insects from one plant to another is easy enough to imagine, but plant diseases may give you another idea. They aren't mobile-like insects, so they can technically jump across plants. What's more, plants don't shake hands, share personal belongings, or sneeze without covering their mouths. So how do plant diseases spread?

There are a lot of ways diseases can get into your garden. For one, you may have bought an infected plant from the nursery. Alternatively, a perching insect or billowing winds may have left your plants the pesky souvenir. Also, there's dormancy with diseases. They could be present one year and go quiet the next, giving the illusion of being gone. However, at that point, all they require to thrive are the right conditions.

Let's talk about the three causal factors of plant diseases (Childs, 2018):

1. **Environmental Factors:** The growth and spread of pathogens can be bolstered by the right climatic conditions. Pathogens usually prefer humid, hot, dry, or cold weather, depending on the type of disease they cause.
2. **Host:** Pathogens require susceptible plant varieties to develop. The plant used might be stressed, malnourished, or unable to fight off the pathogen.
3. **Pathogens:** Pathogens are organisms that prey on vulnerable plants, entering into their system and waiting for favorable conditions. Pathogens usually get into their hosts from the roots, stems, leaves, injuries, or pruning cuts.

Types of Plant Diseases (Childs, 2018):

Anthracnose

Anthracnose is more prevalent in the Eastern regions of the United States. It is fungal in nature and stems from one of the more common plant pathogens: the genus *Colletotrichum*. Plants infected with anthracnose will develop dark and water-soaked lesions on their fruits, leaves, and stems. In the center of these lesions sit pink masses of spores with a gelatinous appearance. Anthracnose is especially popular during warm and moist weather and can ruin large amounts of plants in a matter of days.

Signs and Symptoms

After a cool, wet spring, plants' leaves will usually develop irregular dark blotches. Affected areas may also include twigs and buds and eventually fall off after some days. Symptoms tend to vary across host plants.

Contraction and Spread

Spores hibernate in winter on twigs before developing in cool and wet weather. Propagation is usually by air.

Susceptible Plants

Small ornamental trees, such as dogwood are easily susceptible to anthracnose. Other plants favored by the pathogen are trees like maple, ash, and sycamore.

Potential Outcome and Diagnosis

It's unlikely that anthracnose will result in the death of the plant outright. However, the constant defoliation may result in unsightly plants.

Managing Anthracnose

- You want to grow your crops in well-aerated areas and religiously prune thick crowns and foliage to improve air circulation.
- When buying plants, study their tags and search for resistant varieties.
- Fertilize your plants regularly to encourage the rapid growth of new foliage.

Crown Rot

Crown rot is a common plant disease in North America. Its pathogen is a soilborne fungus, which can thrive in the soil indefinitely. This feature makes it persistent. It often thrives in heavy conditions and wet weather. Although symptoms may vary across plants, once the disease occurs, the chances of survival for plants are low.

Signs and Symptoms

Plants will develop mushy stems and yellowing foliage above the ground. Symptoms may start showing at any point within the growing period, although it's more likely to occur during hot and humid weather. Otherwise known as the southern blight, crown rot can be fatal to plants.

Contraction and Spread

Organisms that cause crown rot typically live around the soil's surface, waiting for an entryway to possess a host plant and wreck its tissue system.

Susceptible Plants

Plants like daylilies, phloxes, hostas, bleeding hearts, and other perennials are victims of crown rot.

Possible Outcome and Diagnosis

If left unchecked or untreated, crown rot can quickly kill a plant, but it doesn't end there. If it succeeds, the organism can become a recurring problem in your growing area.

Managing Crown Rot

- Plants infected with crown rot should not be included in compost piles or bins, as the pathogen will keep thriving in the compost and pose a much bigger problem in the future.
- Dig up infected plants and remove about 12 inches of soil off the top of where infected plants used to be.
- Fungicides like Terrachlor might save your plants. However, the timing of the application is

essential. Once the crown has completely rotted, there's no saving the plant anymore.

- Bury infected plants in a hole several feet deep to prevent the spread of spores.

Black Spot

Black spot is a common occurrence to many plants and can be caused by various fungi of genera *Stigmea, Glomerella, Placosphaeria, Asterina, Schizothyrium, Diplotheca, Gnomonia*, and *Asterinella*. Infection rates are highest during damp weather and will present round or irregular black spots. Leaves are the most common areas affected by black spots, although they can sometimes be found on susceptible plants' flower parts, stems, and petioles.

Signs and Symptoms

Black spots will usually appear on stems and leaves of plants during spring. At this point, the spots are small and can be easily missed. However, by summer, the spots become larger, resulting in the yellowing and falling off of leaves.

Contraction and Spread

Fungus spores hibernate in winter on the stems and leaves of plants that touch the soil. Water splashes help spread the fungus to young leaves and stems from spring to fall.

Susceptible Plants

Roses are the primary victims of black spots.

Potential Outcome and Diagnosis

As old leaves wither and fall off, new leaves will grow in their place. The process repeats itself, making the plant weaker and vulnerable to other insects and pathogens. What's more, the disease makes an unsightly appearance of the plant.

Managing Black Spots

- Get some fungicides from your local garden center. Don't wait until symptoms appear to apply it.
- Plant your roses in well-aerated areas that are farther from plants that block the flow of air.
- Prune infected leaves once spots begin to appear.
- Purchase resistant varieties for your garden.
- Refrain from wetting the leaves of your plants, especially during the later periods of the day.

Rust

There are over 5,000 recorded varieties of rusts that affect plants. *Phragmidium spp.,* or common rust, is a fungal disease that preys on plants like tomatoes, daylilies, snapdragons, roses, beans, lawns, and hollyhocks. They tend to favor mature plants, and symptoms will manifest on the surface of lower-placed leaves. Rust diseases thrive in four to eight hours of moisture (rain, dew, or humidity), warm temperatures, and low light intensity; they also thrive in up to 16 hours of high temperatures, high light intensity, and the slow drying of the surfaces of leaves.

Signs and Symptoms

Infected plants usually exhibit powdery brown or rusty-orange spots on both sides of their leaves. The disease is most common during fall and summer, although it doesn't specifically stick to these periods.

Contraction and Spread

Water and wind are the primary propagators of spores, particularly in humid conditions.

Susceptible Plants

Rust typically affects peonies, mums, geraniums, snapdragons, and asters.

Potential Outcome and Diagnosis

Although this disease doesn't outrightly kill the plant, it weakens plant systems and decreases the production of fruit and flowers.

Managing Rust

- When buying plants, study the labels and opt for resistant varieties. If you must grow a susceptible variety, consult your local garden center for fungicides to use during the early periods of summer to prevent infection.
- Prune and destroy affected areas of plants.
- Ensure that plant foliage is dry at all times during irrigation.
- Remove dense vegetation from around plants to improve air circulation.

Botrytis Gray Mold

The gray mold affects a wide array of plants. It is a fungal disease that quickly moves through gardens, especially in cool, damp, or mild weather. This disease typically appears on leaves, produce, and flowers in the form of soft, mushy, and grayish spots. In high humidity, spores may be covered with coatings of gray fungal spores. Affected plants and fruits will typically rot, become shriveled, or exhibit black, stone-like sclerotia, which is a dense mass of solidified fungal filaments. Gray mold can be found near the soil's surface or within the areas of plants with the densest foliage.

Signs and Symptoms

In spring, affected plants will develop wet-looking spots on tender blossoms and new flower buds. Over time, it might spread to the stems and leaves. Fruits are not spared in the attack and will most likely become susceptible in wet and cool weather. Spots develop and grow larger with gray fuzz covering.

Contraction and Spread

Rain and wind help to propagate gray mold spores, which thrive in cool and wet weather.

Susceptible Plants

There are almost no limits to the type of plants affected by the botrytis gray mold.

Potential Outcome and Diagnosis

Fruits spoil and rot; plants grow weaker over time, and flower buds refuse to bloom.

Managing Botrytis Gray Mold

- You want to plant your crops in areas with plenty of air circulation.
- Remove and bury infected plants about 18 to 24 inches deep and away from your garden.
- Fungicides can help in the fight against gray mold. Try using Dicloran or Maneb.
- When watering your garden, avoid wetting the foliage or flowers.
- Don't add affected plants to your compost bins or piles.

Cedar-Apple Rust

Gymnosporangium juniperi-virginianae, otherwise known as cedar-apple rust, is caused by a fungal pathogen that thrives best on mature juniper plants that have completed their two-year life cycle. The disease spores and hibernates in winter as reddish-brown galls on the young twigs of many juniper plants. During the early period of spring, as the wet weather sets in, the galls become swollen and turn bright orange. These spores are then carried by wind to crab apple and apple trees, where they begin to develop against the next growing season. After the development process, the spores will only affect junipers. Essentially, the fungus moves from junipers to apples and back to junipers without spreading between apple trees.

Signs and Symptoms

During fall, Eastern red cedars will typically have hard brown galls on their twigs. As spring sets in, the galls will swell and release spores for propagation by the wind. The spores find their way to the foliage of apple trees sometime in late spring. At this point, orange spots grow on the tree's leaves all through the summer month. Midway through summer, infected leaves will fall off, making the tree look like a nightmare.

Contraction and Spread

Galls produce spores in wet spring weather, then carried by wind to apple foliage. As the spores ripen, the wind carries them back to the cedar, where they hibernate to continue the cycle in the next season.

Susceptible Plants

Crab apples, apples, and Eastern red cedar are all highly susceptible to this disease.

Potential Outcome and Diagnosis

Affected plants are dreadful to look at and messy.

Managing Cedar-Apple Rust

- Your garden shouldn't have both apples and Eastern red cedars.
- If you must grow them together, use resistant varieties.
- Susceptible apple trees may benefit from fungicides, so you'll want to spray your trees, especially when flower buds start to bloom.

Powdery Mildew

Powdery mildew is one of the most recognizable and common plant diseases that can be found in every region of the United States. The disease stems from a range of closely related fungi, which have limited host ranges. For instance, the various fungi that affect your roses will not survive on lilacs, so spreading is impossible to other plant types. Powdery mildew thrives in areas with high humidity and low soil moisture. Affected plants will typically exhibit brown leaves, which fall off eventually. The disease avoids mature leaves and will likely prey on young, succulent growth.

Signs and Symptoms

Look for white granular patches with the appearance of dust on the bottom and top of leaves, stems, fruit, and flowers. You can easily rub it off with your fingers. This disease doesn't have a particular period and can spring up at any point during the planting season if susceptible varieties are planted.

Contraction and Spread

Powdery mildew produces spores, which are propagated by the wind.

Susceptible Plants

The disease has quite a range and will affect plants like aster, crab apple, lilac, lungwort, bee balm, phlox, rose, and zinnia.

Potential Outcome and Diagnosis

While powdery mildew may be incapable of killing your plants, it will do some damage to their appearances.

Managing Powdery Mildew

- Ensure your plants are well watered and healthy to prevent stress.
- Apply horticultural oils and fungicides with potassium bicarbonate before searching for mildew. Alternatively, spray them to prevent the spread of diseases to other areas of the plant or similar plants.
- Resistant varieties will save you a lot of hassle.

- Air circulation is crucial when planting susceptible species, so you want to avoid overcrowding plants.

Fire Blight

Fire blight gets its name from its scorched appearance on affected plants. This disease is of bacterial origins (*Erwinia amylovora*) and can be found on members of the rose family, like pears and apples. It accesses its host through the branches, then makes its way down the stem, resulting in dieback. Soft, new growth is the primary prey of fire blight, so dieback is usually found near the tops of affected plants.

Signs and Symptoms

For the most part, infected branches and leaves will turn black or brown. However, the leaves and branches will not fall off even after death. You can also expect reddish, water-soaked lesions on the bark of affected trees. In warm climates, the lesions will leak orange-brown liquid. Fire blight is destructive and can kill plants, limbs, blossoms, shoots, and all.

Contraction and Spread

In winter, the bacteria hibernates in infected barks before spreading via wind, insects, dew, or splashing rain. Warm and moist weather is the perfect propagation period for fire blight, especially during flowering.

Managing Fire Blight

- When you discover fire blight on your plants, immediately prune off the infected parts. Cut from a foot below the infected area and burn the pruned areas to avoid further spreading the pathogen.
- Move your plants away from wild varieties for pear, apple, and hawthorn.
- When pruning, use a 10% bleach or alcohol solution to sterilize the shears between cuts to avoid transferring the pathogen between branches of the same plant.
- Go for resistant varieties of plants for your garden.
- Heavy pruning and excess use of nitrogenous fertilizers can encourage the growth of pathogens.

PESTS

The presence of a single bug in your garden isn't necessarily a problem. Naturally, pests depend on plants for survival, and someone has to grow the plants, right? However, not all their gnawing and chewing necessitates any reaction from you. Even the finest gardens out there have a few bugs, yet their harvests continue to baffle the farmers' market. As a gardener, it's up to you to decide how much pest activity will be allowed on your plants.

To ensure the continued health of your garden, it's best to understand, learn, and know how to identify the baddies of pests. By routine inspection of your crops, you should be able to detect problems easier and faster. The earlier you identify the pests, the easier it is to remove them using organic methods. In this chapter, we'll be looking at a range of invaders you can expect to see in your garden.

Types of Garden Pests

Animals

You have finally set up a stunning garden admired by the neighbors and visitors. Every day, you sit out near it to enjoy the beauty and wonderful fragrance. Well, guess what? You're not the only one intrigued by your garden. The animals in your neighborhood have also seen your garden and babbled about it to their friends. Soon, they'll like to try it for themselves, too.

Deer have the most notoriety for picking the best time to feed on your fine daylilies, hostas, and tulips: when you're out. You can also expect some uncalled visits from wildlife like birds, voles, moles, and woodchucks. These visitors are known for the amount of damage they can cause, leaving behind broken fences, tunnels, and uprooted plants in their wake.

How to Manage Animals

Being able to outsmart the animals that have piqued interest in your garden is a game in itself. Nothing beats the satisfaction of knowing you've beaten them at their own game.

Here are some tips that can help manage the animal issue ("Animal," n.d.):

1. **Identify the Problem:** To keep out the animals, you should find out which ones keep paying courtesy visits to your garden. Creating a higher fence for deer when you have a mole or raccoon problem is about as helpful as patching a leak with a towel.

2. **Set up Protection**: Planting a garden and leaving it unguarded is one way to invite all the animals in. You want to set up physical barriers to keep the critters out. If your garden is plagued by digging rodents, a more effective fencing system may be needed. Rabbits and voles can be diverted by adding a layer of

hardware cloth or chicken wire to the lower ends of your fence.

You'll want the depth of either of these to be three to five inches.

To keep out deer, you'll need a higher fence about eight feet in height. However, this can be costly and leave a dent in your wallet. Another alternative is to use two fences with two to three feet of spacing in between. Deer are claustrophobic and will likely avoid the jump.

1. **Eliminate the Threat:** While it's not recommended to harm the animals, however vile they may be to your garden, you can use traps. Traps are handy for capturing and relocating problematic animals. This should be your final resort if every other alternative fails to work. You want to contact the relevant authorities or a professional who's adept at safely capturing and relocating animals from your area.

2. **Repel the Threat:** Sometimes, the best barriers are invisible to everyone but the animals that you want to keep out. Products like offensive odors, predator urine, and essential oils can be used to ward off pests. Shaking a couple of granules around your

garden will suffice to keep out the unwanted animals, who will sniff the fragrance and get the hint. Remember that rainfall may wear off some of these treatments, so you want to reapply regularly.

Spider Mites

North America hosts most species of spider mites. They have no bias and will feed on indoor and outdoor plants. They are known to cause the most damage in greenhouses. In the real sense of it, spider mites aren't true insects, although they fall under the arachnid classification and have scorpions, ticks, and spiders for relatives. Spider mites typically have a pale or reddish-brown color, with small, oval-shaped bodies.

They exist as colonies and mostly thrive on the bottom of leaves. Spider mites feed on leaf tissues, piercing leaves and slurping up plant fluids. Light dots appear on leaves over time, resulting in yellowing, drying, and eventual fall of affected leaves.

How to Manage Spider Mites

1. Using chemical pesticides will only help spider mites grow in number, as it will kill off the insects that prey on them. Besides, mites have become more resistant to pesticides over time.

As a result, you want to find an effective organic and natural way to deal with them.

2. Hosing down affected plants with strong jets of water can help to decrease the population of spider mites.

3. Prune the infected part of plants, such as stems and leaves. Go beyond physical webbings, and discard them in the garbage. Do not add these to your compost pile. If an entire plant is infested, pull it out to prevent spread to neighboring plants.

4. Invest in natural enemies and predators of the spider mite, like lacewings, ladybugs, and other predatory mites. These are available commercially and are best applied when the spider mites population is still relatively low.

Thrips

Thrips are common pests found in outdoor and indoor gardens and greenhouses. They cause damage by sucking out plant juices and scraping at leaves, flowers, and fruits. Infested plants will usually develop a pale color before turning splotchy, then silvery. These plants will start to look contorted, scarred, and discolored and will eventually die.

Thrips are incredibly active pests and usually feed as a group. When disturbed, they fly or leap off the plant. Common prey of this pest are flowers like roses and gladioli, and foods like carrots, onions, beans, and squash, among others. Both the wingless larvae and mature adults prefer blossoms in the light colors spectrum, such as yellow and white. They are the primary propagators of impatiens necrotic spot virus and tomato spotted wilt virus.

How to Manage Thrips

1. Removing grass and weeds from around your garden can help remove potential hosts.
2. Evaluate every plant before introducing it into your garden. Check for signs of thrips and their effects on plants.
3. Hose down plants with strong, ambient water to lower insect population.
4. Discard infested plants by bagging them up and throwing them in the garbage. Do not add these to your compost.
5. Clear out crop debris from your garden, particularly onion leaves post-harvest.
6. Avoid using green mulch, as they attract thrips. Go for dry mulch instead.
7. Invest in commercially available predators of

thrips, such as ladybugs, lacewings, and pirate bugs.

Whitefly

Whiteflies make their homes in greenhouses, indoor plants, and tomatoes. They depend on the sap produced by plants, which they suck in hordes from the bottom of leaves. Disturbing infested plants will result in winged adults taking to the air momentarily before returning to the plant. Both adults and nymphs feed on the new growth of plants by sucking out their juices.

This leads to lower yields, yellowing of leaves, and stunted growth. Whiteflies make plants weaker and more vulnerable to diseases. Like aphids, whiteflies are known to secret honeydew on host plants, resulting in black sooty molds and sticky leaves. They are also well-known propagators of many viruses that affect plants.

How to Manage Whiteflies

1. When dealing with high populations of whiteflies, consider using short-lived, organic pesticides with low toxicity. After, introduce predators to aid population control, like lacewing and ladybug, which feed on the parasites and eggs of the whitefly. These

predators are best used when the whitefly population is between low to medium.

2. Infested plants can be hosed down with strong jets of water to lower the pest population.
3. Use yellow sticky traps to check and reduce the adult population.

Pill Bug and Sow Bug

These insects can be found in landscaped areas and home gardens across the United States. Otherwise known as roly-poly bugs, these insects are usually scavengers, meaning their primary food source is decaying matter. This makes them valuable players in the decomposition cycle. Albeit, if the population is high, food would run out faster. To make up for this shortage, they will usually resort to feeding on the fruits, leaves, new roots, and seedlings of plants, especially those directly on or close to the soil. They'd scurry away to safety when disturbed, seeking safety in damp and dark areas such as garden debris, underneath rocks and leaves, and in mulch.

How to Manage Pill Bugs and Sow Bugs

1. Consider introducing insect killer granules to landscaped areas, lawns, and foundations to fend off or eliminate these troublesome pests.

2. Go for mulch with a coarse texture that allows better water absorption. This will ensure that the surface around plants stays damp only momentarily.

3. Roly-poly bugs can be reduced by eliminating potential habitats that encourage the species' growth. Clear out leaf piles, weeds, garden debris, and fallen fruits near your garden.

4. Increase air circulation around your plants. Use a trellis for your vines and raise fruits, such as melons, strawberries, and beans off the ground.

Leaf Miner

These pests can be found in landscaped areas, home gardens, and greenhouses. Their names are characteristic of how they destroy plants: by moving within leaves. Leaf miners are the larvae of insects that feed on the midpoint of leaves. Infested plants will usually have around six or more larvae on each leaf. While the damage caused by this pest can lead to a decrease in yield, healthier plants can survive and recover over time. Common host plants for leaf miners are ornamental crops, beans, lettuce, citrus trees, peppers, shrubs, cabbage, and blackberry.

How to Manage Leaf Miners

1. Study your plants closely. All initial signs of tunneling should be investigated. If infested, squeezing the tunnel between your fingers should kill the larvae. Early detection will result in better survival rates for your plants.
2. Invest in floating row covers to keep flies from laying their eggs on your crops.
3. Blue and yellow sticky traps work well for catching adults that lay eggs.
4. Prune and destroy infested leaves and plants from your garden.
5. *Diglyphus isaea*, the parasitic wasp, is a well-known predator of leaf miners and can be obtained from your local gardening supplies store. This wasp comes in handy for your ornamental and vegetable garden, whether indoors or outdoors.
6. Cover the area surrounding infested plants with plastic mulches. This will prevent the eggs from becoming pupae after reaching the ground.

PESTICIDES

For a healthy, thriving garden complete with vibrant plants, insect pests can be a nightmare to have around. The most frustrating outcome is finding your labor of love brought to ruin by pests that put no effort in. To avoid this, you may want to invest in some insecticides, but you don't want to get just any type of insecticide. You want to get an eco-friendly, organic insecticide that isn't full of toxic chemicals that can harm your plants or you.

Forms of Pesticide

Botanical Pesticides

In contrast to artificial insecticides made with chemicals that are harmful to humans, the environment, and plants, botanical insecticides are made with natural chemicals obtained from minerals or plants. While these insecticides are relatively safer for plants and humans, they are devastating for insects and diseases. Here are some botanical pesticides you might consider for your garden (MorningChores Staff, n.d.):

1. **Essential Plant Oils:** Essential oils are a crucial element in several botanical insecticides and repellents. Some common examples of these oils are soybean, eucalyptus, rosemary, pennyroyal, lavender, citronella,

peppermint, and cedar oils. Their chemical properties make them effective at wading off a vast array of insects that may be harmful to your plants while causing little to no problems to pets, people, and the environment.

2. Pyrethrin-Based Insecticides: Pyrethrin is an extract obtained from the chrysanthemum's flowers. The insecticide has shown profound effects in keeping away wasps, scales, cockroaches, beetles (particularly the Japanese beetle), caterpillars, bugs, fleas, ants, flies, and aphids.

Pyrethrin-based insecticides are ideal for organic gardening, as they easily dissipate after application from both soil and plants, especially after the pests are defeated. They have low toxicity levels and are safe to use around people, livestock, and pets. Pyrethrin is quick-acting and will knock out insects soon after application. However, insects may survive if the dose you apply isn't high enough.

3. Neem Oil: Neem oil is obtained naturally from the seeds and fruits of the neem tree, which are in some parts of Asia, particularly India. In English, the tree is known as the margosa tree, which is a botanical name of *Azadirachta indica*. The oil obtained from the tree usually has a yellowish or dark brown tone, a smell comparable to sulfur or garlic, and a bitter taste. Apart from its insect-repellent qualities, Neem oil is also medicinal and found in hair and skin care products.

4. Spinosad: Unlike the other types of botanical insecticides, Spinosad does not have a direct source. It is obtained from the combination of Spinosyn A and Spinosyn B, which are naturally occurring chemicals created by soil bacterium. The chemicals are toxic to insects hence the effectiveness of Spinosad as an insect repellant.

When insects come into contact with the repellent, which can be in the form of a spray, dust, or granule, it destroys their nervous system. As a result, insects become paralyzed and can only survive for one to two days. Gruesome, maybe, but you'd rather it was them than your plants.

Chemical Pesticides

Chemical pesticides are commonly used in rural and urban environments and for domestic or commercial purposes. They usually take the form of herbicides, rodenticides, fungicides, or insecticides. All three forms aim to control and stop diseases and pests that affect plants. While usage can be interchangeable, their purposes are distinct in and of themselves. They include (MorningChores Staff, n.d.):

1. **Herbicides:** Herbicides are designed to eliminate unwanted plants from your garden (case in point, weeds). While herbicides can be made to eradicate only one type of plant, some hold no bias and will kill all plants it comes in contact with. When buying these, you want to study the label properly and be careful with your application.

2. **Rodenticides and Fungicides:** Pesticides have a wider range than insecticides because they are designed as repellents for pests in general, meaning they help to keep diseases, pathogens (bacteria, fungus, and virus), animals (slugs, snails, etcetera), and insects away. Pesticides are deadly to the touch and ingestion of the pests that they repel, and they have a longer-lasting potency period. Although, that factor also depends on the concentration level of the pesticide during application.

3. **Insecticides:** Insecticides are a more specific type of pesticide that targets insects. Some may also include baits for snails, wasps, and ants. Others may come in the form of sprays that affect various insects. Insecticides can also be used for managing insect infestation from the larvae before growth occurs and the adult emerges.

Precautions for Using Pesticides

- Make sure to study the instructions on every pesticide you buy. Some may even come with manuals for a step-by-step guide. Follow the outlines of the producer.
- If you get some pesticide on your hands, even if they are botanical or eco-friendly, ensure to wash your hands thoroughly with soap and water. Failing to do so might result in a rash. If you still get a rash after washing your hands, discontinue using the product and consider visiting your doctor.
- Before using pesticides, dress the part. Wear long sleeves, gloves, and full-length pants. You want to strap on a mask to protect your eyes and nose from the fumes. Even organic products may affect sensitive skin or cause breathing issues once opened.

How to Avoid Future Pest Problems

There are many hacks and tips you can consider to manage the recurrence of pest problems in your garden. Let's take a look at a few:

1. When buying plants for your garden, perform a thorough inspection before finalizing the

purchase. You don't want to invite problems to your garden.

2. Steer clear of varieties that are easily susceptible to pests and diseases. For instance, the indica variety of myrtle and crape are more vulnerable to aphid attacks than their contemporaries. If your garden is full of Japanese beetles, you're better off going for ornamental crops that are of no use to them. Think silver and red maples, rhododendron, flowering dogwood, lilac, and boxwood.

3. After pruning the garden, clear out leaf litter, weeds, piles of stone, excess mulch, and debris. Leaving these around will only give pests hiding places to pick apart your plants.

4. Healthy and vigorous plants can better manage attacks from pests and diseases. Stressed plants, on the other hand, are more susceptible. You want to cater to your plants properly, providing enough water, fertilizer, sunlight, and air. Sometimes, all you need to keep pests and diseases at bay are the right conditions. For instance, spider mites will likely infest plants when the weather is dry and hot. Well-watered plants are less likely to be invaded during this period.

5. Don't let minor problems grow out of hand.

Take your time to investigate your plants and prune infested areas, like branches and leaves. If possible, handpick insects off your plants. Handpicking is best done during the early morning hours when the weather is relatively cooler and pests are inactive. A strong jet of water may also suffice to wash pests like aphids, scales, and spider mites off your plants.

6. Be careful when using pesticides; you don't want to eliminate all the pests. Some are good and can help control the population of harmful invaders. For instance, parasitic wasps, minute pirate bugs, praying mantises, and ladybugs feed on insects that damage plants. Predatory mites, minute pirate bugs, and lacewing larvae are predators of spider mites; ladybugs prey on aphids, and parasitic wasps ward off scales. Bees also play a role in the garden by pollinating flowers without directly harming your crops.

7

STEP 7- SEASONAL TASKS AND MAINTENANCE

SPRING TASKS AND SPRING BLOOMS

Spring is the peak of the gardening season because plant life begins anew after the frost of winter. It's the time when you have to gear up and get into the garden—armed with the necessary tools to clean out your growing area—set up your beds, prune perennial crops that have overwintered, make necessary repairs, and begin the growing season cheerfully.

This section covers step-by-step guidelines for preparing for the new growing season. First, we'll start with spring (Martin, n.d.-a):

1. Begin With a Round of Inspection: To fix what is broken, you must know it's broken. During the early days of spring, just as the weather starts to warm up, go into your garden with a notepad and your inspector's hat. The time is right to find out how winter treated your garden while you were indoors. Here are some things you want to take note of:

- Signs of animal burrowing: rabbits, voles, chipmunks, skunks, moles, or groundhogs may have taken the liberty to hibernate in your garden. You want to find these hideouts so that your fresh plants don't become their first meal. Check for damages by rodents or deer, especially on woody plants.
- Evaluate your beds and find out if they need cleaning out.
- Check for damages on perennials by snow, ice, or cold.
- Inspect hardscaping elements that are broken, bowing, or rotten—think benches, trellises, walls, sheds, and fences.

2. Start the Cleaning Process: Once you've noted down all that needs fixing, the next step is to begin the cleaning process. The sooner you begin, the better. You want to have your garden tidy before spring bulbs start to emerge. Clean out plant debris from your growing beds, including perennial foliage from the previous year, matted down leaves, fallen branches, annuals you failed to remove the previous season, perennial hibiscus, and ornamental grasses. One way to achieve healthy plants is to maintain good hygiene in your garden.

If you have a water feature, like a pond or fountain, you also want to clean them out and remove debris that may have gotten in. After, clean and sterilize your containers and birdbaths before reintroducing them into the garden. A bleach and water mixture should help disinfect any lingering insect eggs or diseases.

3. Check Your Soil: Winter may have done a number on your growing area, so it's best to inspect your soil before planting. Soil testing is recommended every three to five years to identify the organic materials and nutrients that may be missing or excessive in your garden.

For instance, a soil test might show that your garden is high in nitrogen, meaning you'd be better off using fertilizers with little nitrogen content. You may also find your garden has high alkalinity. This would mean aluminum sulfate may be necessary for your acid-loving plants (e.g., hydrangeas) and evergreens. Visit the extension service website of your state to find more on how to collect soil samples and submit them for testing.

4. Improve the Nutrient Content of Your Soil: After receiving the evaluation for your soil sample, you want to consult a professional at your local garden center. You'll get expert advice on the best products for your soil type and how to achieve healthy crops. As a rule of thumb, when feeding your soil, spread one or two inches of compost as a topdress, including manure and humus.

This should be done during the early periods of spring. Also, add a sprinkle of organic, slow-release plant food around your overwintered shrubs and perennials. Earthworms and other tiny burrowing animals will break down and pull the organic materials into the soil over time.

5. Start Setting up Support Systems Like Stakes and Trellises: If you took your trellises indoors during the winter months, you might want to bring them back out and start setting up again with the new season. Inspect and ensure that they are sturdy. If necessary, give them a new coat of fresh paint before setting up. If you will be growing perennials that require some form of support, now's the right time to get them out and set them up. Otherwise, it'll be much harder to set up once the plants start blooming again.

6. Set Up Your Spring Borders and Containers: While many annual crops are best grown when the soil has warmed up slightly, some plants favor the fading chill of winter and won't mind early cultivation, like daisies (*Osteospermum* variety), nemesia, and pansies. Get out your spring containers to grow some early spring plants. For the other annuals that prefer warmer soils, hold off until the final frost date of your area.

7. Transplant Shrubs and Split Up Perennials: Just as the perennials are reviving and bulbs start to pop, split up your perennials and transplant them, especially ones that are mature enough to be divided or have outgrown their growing area. For the most part, it is best to do your splitting and transplanting during the seasons they are not in bloom. For instance, fall and summer bloomers are best split and transplanted in spring, and spring bloomers should be done in fall. This way, their bloom cycles are unaffected, and they get enough time to settle in.

For evergreen shrubs, the best transplanting period is during the early periods of spring, just before new growth begins to show. Alternatively, they could be done earlier during fall to allow their roots enough time to be established against winter. For deciduous shrubs, the best time is before or after they bloom when the weather is mild, although they tend to adapt better when transplanted in fall and spring. Dormant periods are preferable for transplanting because plants are less likely to be stressed by the ordeal; they will adapt better and recover quickly.

8. Prepare Your Covers for When Freezing Temperatures Arise: If you live in a region that experiences late freezing and frosts in spring, you may want to prepare some cover for your plants, particularly for new foliage and buds. Keep an eye on the forecast. However, no covering is needed if the buds are yet to open. Use towels and old sheets for cover, or you could get garden row covers from your local garden supplies store. Under no circumstances should you use tarpaulins or plastic sheets to cover your plants. Plastic is more likely to magnify the effect of frost instead of mitigating it, which is detrimental to the emerging foliage and buds.

9. Get Pruning: Spring is the perfect time to prune the woody trees and shrubs in your garden. Follow the tips and tricks below for how to go about pruning after winter:

- Evergreen plants can be sheared in spring, especially after their first bout of new growth has fully emerged.
- As a rule of thumb, trim flowering shrubs emerging from new wood. This includes crops that flower during the summer, such as roses, rose of Sharon, potentilla, butterfly bush,

panicle hydrangea, and smooth hydrangea. Flower buds will typically appear after pruning with a flush of new growth.

- Plants damaged or broken by cold, snow, and ice should be pruned. Deadwood should also be removed.
- Early flowering shrubs should be left alone, together with plants that bloom on old wood (i.e., stems from the previous season), such as lilac, weigela, forsythia, azalea, quince, and ninebark. Pruning may result in cutting off the flower buds of the new season. While the plants may not appear like it, the buds are present.

10. Tackle Hardscaping Issues: During the early periods of spring, just before you start tilling the ground and planting your crops, focus on hardscaping. You want to fix your raised beds, window boxes, sheds, benches, trellises, decks, retaining walls, and fences. Next, clean your gutters and level any stepping-stones around. Hardscaping is one of the easiest parts of spring cleaning, as plants are usually still dormant for the most part. In addition, you can leverage the time to execute new raised beds, increase old ones, and take care of the edges. If the temperature is right, you can slap on a new coat of paint and seal or stain wooden hardscaping materials.

SUMMER TASKS AND SUMMER BLOOMS

In summer, the sun is out, the weather is warm, and your labor of love during spring starts to pay off. As you enjoy the outcome of your efforts, here are some chores to tackle in your garden to ensure healthy and vibrant plants for the rest of the growing season (Martin, 2019):

1. Keep the Weeds Out: Weeds grow faster than actual plants, so it helps to stay on top of the situation at all times. Inspect your garden regularly, and at the first sight of weeds, pull them out and dispose of them properly. Catch them before they start seeding to prevent propagation around your garden. Check beneath your crops for weed undergrowth.

2. Introduce a Splash of Color in Your Garden: Regardless of the number of plants you procured at the nursery or garden center, there's almost always an area of your garden that may be lacking color vibrancy, especially in summer. It could be your border crops that bloom in spring or a pot of cool-season bloomers that are past their flowering period. Whatever the case, it remains a patch of green for a good part of the season. If you likely entertain guests in your garden, you may want to spice up the colors.

When picking plants for the summer season, consider getting heat-tolerant varieties. These take their time to settle during the summer months and will bloom in time to add splotches of color to your garden.

3. Keep an Eye Out for Pests: Insects and other pests are usually most active during summer, so you want to be watchful for when they show up. Early detection is critical. Some gardeners don't mind visitors like the Japanese beetle, slugs, grasshoppers, and snails. However, it's your decision how you want to manage what comes into your garden.

During the summer months, take your time to apply pesticides and repellents. If you put up any during spring, a touch-up should suffice. Monitor the growth rate of your plants because pests may attack at different levels. For instance, repellents sprayed around the base of a plant may not work on a deer problem if they eat from the top of the plant, so you want to use sprays higher up. Consider using granular repellents around the base to keep off pests that attack from below, like rabbits, moles, voles, etc.

4. Check Your Mulch: Mulch doesn't last forever, particularly finely-textured ones which tend to wear off before the end of the season. Reapplication is necessary to continuously maintain the temperature of the roots for plants and help conserve moisture in the soil. This prevents the plants from being stressed and suffering due to the summer heat. Since uncultivated areas of the garden are also covered, mulch serves as weed management. Pick up some more mulch to cover up thinning areas or bare spots in your garden.

5. Prune Finished Perennial Blossoms: Many annual varieties tend to self-clean, saving you the effort and time otherwise used to clean out faded blossoms. However, it's a different story with perennials, which are prone to deadheading. This means that you'd need to prune spent flower stems to improve the look of the plant and encourage bloom.

For instance, *Dianthus* plants thrive better when their spent flowers are sheared post-summer. Not only do they look neater, but the prettier foliage is exposed, and the plant gets to bloom again just as fall sets in. Deadheading dianthus can be done with shears. Trim off flower stems down to the topmost part of its mounded foliage. You can prune other plants this way for reblooming during or after summer.

In the same vein, spent flower stalks from flowers such as bee balm, phlox, hostas, daylilies, salvia, or daisies can be pruned to improve the plants' looks. In most cases, the plants may even go on to experience bloom again. For some plants, you're better off leaving spent flower stems on. For example, the Decadence brand

Baptisia plants grow the pods from the same place as the flowers, so if you need those pods, pruning those stems would mean the end of them.

6. Provide Leaning Plants With Support: Over time, your plants will mature, and they may begin to wobble in the breeze or lean on neighboring plants. While it's not inherently bad, a support system could be of help to your plants. Leaning might lead to overcrowding, which means decreased aeration and sunlight; thus, it creates a breeding ground for pests and diseases. Leaning plants may also break if not managed well. There are many support systems to pick from, including rings, support cages, and poles. These can be found at your local garden supplies store. You may want to invest in more support for climbing plants, especially those that have used up spaces on their trellises. Also, get some garden twine to help hold plants to the supports.

7. Make Provisions for Your Feathered Visitors: Birds are a great addition to any garden. They don't just make it livelier and more colorful, but their songs and antics may offer good entertainment. Birds feed on bugs, so they also help manage pests that would otherwise harm your plants. If you have a bird feeder or birdbath, ensure that you keep it sanitary. Clean it regularly to keep off germs and pathogens. Your birdbath should contain freshwater, and it should be next to a water source, like a sprinkler head, which fills it as the birds use it up. You may also want to put off deadheading your plants for a while, especially those that produce seeds that birds feed on, like sunflowers.

8. Plants Annuals in Empty Spots: After removing the foliage of dormant spring bulbs and clearing out weeds, your garden may open up with several patches of space. Your best bet is to fill these spaces with annuals. They have shallow roots and will likely have completed their life cycles before the turn of the new growing year. Consider saving some annuals for the summer months to plant in spaces that show up in the garden. The new plants will add to the overall beauty of the area.

AUTUMN TASKS AND AUTUMN BLOOMS

Here are some tips to help with the fall season and its new list of tasks ("10 Fall Gardening Tasks to Make Your Garden Sing Next Spring," n.d.):

1. Perform Garden Evaluations: Take note of the plants that went according to plan in the previous growing season. Are they worth repeating? Also, make an entry of the plants you want to get during your next shopping trip for autumn planting.

This is arguably the best time to evaluate factors like:

- Areas to grow plants that favor fall and are pleasing to the eye
- The number of plants that should be split up and transplanted
- Plants that need moving to better areas within the garden
- Areas that require privacy or protection against pests and privacy concerns

2. It's Planting Time: The soil is relatively warm in autumn, and the air is just starting to cool. These conditions are perfect for planting, as they foster the growth of healthy roots in plants that see out their life cycles. Your local garden center may have an end-of-season sale at this point, so you'll want to stock up on perennials to plant in your garden. You want to time your planting period around six weeks before the ground freezes to allow roots to settle nicely into the soil.

3. Remove the Annuals From Your Garden: Annuals have had their chance. They've had a great run, but when autumn rolls in, it's time to say goodbye and start making preparations for winter. Clearing out annuals can be a chore, especially as some of them may still be

174 | SANDY NEWTON

experiencing bloom well into fall. However, it'd be a shame for frost to catch up with them because they'll wither away and be twice as much work to clean up. If the plants are still healthy, you can add them to your compost. This way, you won't feel like you gave them up.

4. Cut Back Some Perennials: As your perennials become dormant in anticipation of winter, now might be a good time to clean up their foliage and tidy your garden beds. Many gardeners will usually prune foliage down to ground level. This pruning system works well, especially for plants that have been attacked by pests like slugs, as they will often lay eggs on dormant foliage. Taking off the entire foliage will reduce potential slug attacks in the future. Avoid pruning shrubs at this time.

Other perennials you shouldn't prune:

- Winter-loving perennials such as Lenten roses, false indigo, ornamental onion, coneflowers, autumn joy stonecrop, and ornamental grasses.
- Woody-stemmed perennials such as butterfly bush, Russian sage, rose mallow, and lavender.
- Semi-evergreens and evergreen perennials such as bugleweed, coral bells, foamflower, creeping phlox, red hot poker, pinks, and foamy bells.

5. Clean Up Leaves and Add Mulch: Autumn is nature's mulching process, with the leaves of deciduous trees covering the ground. These leaves, with their delicate textures, like honey locust and willow trees, will degrade over time and may not require any form of raking.

However, broader leaves like oak, sycamore, and maple cover the ground, taking longer to decompose fully if left untouched. This way, weeds are smothered, allowing less competition for nutrients in your garden. During the early periods of fall, rake these broad leaves and store them for later. Using them as mulch during late fall, just as winter starts to set in, will protect your garden by insulating overwintering crops, killing weeds, and adding nutrients to the soil as they decompose.

6. Do Away With Infected Foliage: Although you can include the prune parts of some plants into your compost pile, infected foliage is a definite no. This is because compost piles may not heat up enough to kill pathogens. Pick up all the infected foliage, seal them in a bag, and toss them to avoid reintroducing infection.

7. Take Care of Newly Planted and Sensitive Crops: If you want to push the hardiness limits of some plants, it may help to cover them in evergreen boughs with shredded leaves, especially as they begin to lie dormant.

Doing this will keep them warm through the winter. The same can be done for crops with extra sensitive buds, such as some *Hydrangea macrophylla* cultivars.

In addition, consider adding mulch to your newly planted perennials, particularly those whose root systems haven't fully developed. Doing this helps keep the plants form and prevent the plant from heaving from the ground as the soil thaws and freezes over winter. Mulch allows for better consistency in soil temperature, providing an extra layer of protection for plants against pest attacks.

8. Get Creative: When autumn comes around, creativity is the order of the day. Consider taking dried flowers and cut branches from your garden to decorate your house. Winter is at hand, anyway, so you want to have a good time even if you are snowed in. Crops such as ornamental grass plumes, berried branches, hydrangea flowers, and other plants containing seed pods can provide you with some indoor creativity.

WINTER TASKS AND WINTER BLOOMS

You are less likely to be out as winter grows stronger, so you want to get things done quickly. Setting up your garden for spring is a good idea and can save you lots of work when the new planting season comes around.

Here are some activities you can get started on in winter (West Coast Gardens, 2019):

1. Take Care of Finished or Rotting Plants: Aside from making your garden look like a mess, old and rotting plants can be a breeding site for pathogens, diseases, and pests. It's not uncommon for insects to lay eggs on the leaves and stalks of branches. Spent plants, like annuals that have seen out their life cycles, should be removed and buried or discarded away from the garden. For diseased or infected ones, binding them may be the best option. Only bury healthy plants to improve the organic content of the soil and boost general plant well-being.

2. Deal With Weed Invasion That May Spread After Winter: Weeds can be tough to deal with, especially when they are left untouched for a longer duration. You don't want to leave weeds in your garden until spring. Deal with them now. Dig them up and discard them appropriately via binning or burning. Adding them to your compost pile may be problematic, as some weeds remain viable even then. You're better off disposing of weeds entirely than trying to repurpose them. For weeds that don't do well in winter, residual seeds or undergrowth will be killed off before the turn of spring, giving you a fresh, growing lot to work with.

3. Ready the Soil for the Planting Season: While it's common practice to leave soil preparation until spring, getting a head start just before winter rolls around is an excellent way to set up your garden and keep overwintering plants alive. Make your soil amendments at this point, adding compost and fertilizer. Doing this will promote the breaking down of nutrients in time for the planting season. That said, when spring rolls in, you won't have to wait for your soil to warm up to prepare it for planting. Think of it as cleaning your house before going on a trip. You'll return to a clean house and won't have to immediately jump in and work on your return.

4. Prune Your Perennials: Before the chill finally descends and everywhere becomes blanketed in snow, take the time to trim your perennials. Ensure to trim the correct ones that won't suffer as a result. While some flowers may do with a bit of winter pruning, others tend to continue nursing their crowns well into winter. Read the description for the plants or consult with a professional at your local garden center for more information on the plants that may benefit from winter pruning. Whatever the case, clean garden beds and their surrounding areas are necessary. After pruning, you want to clear out the waste as soon as possible, including spent or infected plant parts.

5. Split and Cultivate Your Bulbs: While spring bulbs must have bloomed and gone dormant in preparation for winter, some flowering bulbs, such as lilies may experience a later flowering period. Three to four weeks after this bloom, you want to dig up the bulbs of straggly or crowded plants and split them. But that's not all: These spring bulbs aren't nearly as straightforward as other bulbs, whose locations are usually quite obvious. You may need to do some digging, which can be anywhere between four to eight feet beneath the grown stalk of the plant. As you dig, be careful to loosen the soil. Avoid tugging at the plant. Gently pick up the bulbs and separate bulblets to be transplanted in another area of the garden. If you have already dug up some spring bulbs, it may be the right time to replant them.

6. Gather and Restart Your Compost Bin or Pile: With the warmth of summer away and the chill setting in, microbes will slowly grow dormant as they hibernate during the winter. At this point, it's easy to forget your compost pile or bin. You won't be doing any planting for a while anyway. However, you would have missed a great opportunity. For one, your summer compost has likely run its course and is now ready for use. Applying the compost to your garden beds will begin the process of amending deficiencies in the soil, improving nutrient levels, and overall regenerating the soil before plants form to life again in spring.

Also, with the former compost used up, you can get started on a new batch to see you through the new growing season. Not to worry about the dormant microbes: Insulating your compost bin can keep the microbes up for a little while to help start the composting process. What's more, the leaves and garden wastes from autumn will serve as your base ingredients for the compost.

7. Retouch the Mulch in Your Garden: Mulching in winter holds the same benefit as mulching in summer. The point is to protect your garden from erosion, prevent the growth of weeds, and keep the soil warm. However, there's more to winter mulching. Your garden soil will experience freezing and thawing during the winter months—a cycle that may be devastating for overwintering plants due to heaving and churning. With a thick layer of mulch covering the surface of your garden, the temperature of the soil will be more favorable for plants, and there will be enough moisture to see them through to the next season.

You want to get the mulch around the root of your crops and other important spots in the garden. Additionally, the mulch will likely break down and further improve the soil. You have to be watchful to notice when this happens and top off your garden with more mulch.

8. Evaluate the Plants in Your Garden, and Rate Your Previous Season: How did your garden fare in the previous season? Did your varieties turn out well? You want to take note of these questions to identify under-performing plants and check for types that will do better in your garden. If a plant performs well, you can still go the extra mile to get varieties that bloom earlier.

When analyzing the performance of your flowers, you should take note of those that were attacked by pests or diseases. Check for other factors such as weather, plant placement, moisture, and soil fertility. Record your observations in a note for brainstorming later on. Identify lessons learned and find better ways to improve your garden.

9. Clean and Store Your Tools: Cleaning and oiling your tools regularly during the growing season can be a chore. However, you won't be using them for a while during the winter, so it's best to store them in optimal conditions. Wash your tools to remove grime, debris, and dirt. For ones that can be sharpened, sharpen them using a whetstone or mill file. Finally, before storing them, coat the surface with oil. Use machine oil and a rag or foam. Oiling is meant to prevent rust caused by moisture and oxidation. Doing so will extend the life span of your tools further.

CONCLUSION

Creating your dream flower garden can be simultaneously overwhelming and exciting as a beginner. It's exciting to want to get started right away, but this venture may wear you out if you begin without having the right guide. For most people, the idea of a guide might seem tedious and overly technical—putting them off the thrill of growing their flower garden.

But this book is a simple, fun, and effective gardening guide for beginners that discusses many of the relevant issues of flower gardening. It is especially helpful as it was written after extensive research on the garden practices of experts.

Flower Gardening—In 7 Simple Steps focused on the often overlooked areas of flower gardening. For instance, this book explained critical gardening processes like planning, planting, pruning, soil tests, and determining plant hardiness.

Use the knowledge in this guide to create a garden lush with beautiful and healthy flowers.

If you enjoyed this book, please do leave a review on Amazon.

REFERENCES

10 Fall Gardening Tasks to Make Your Garden Sing Next Spring. (n.d.). Proven Winners. https://www. provenwinners.com/learn/fall/10-fall-gardening-tasks-make-your-garden-sing-next-spring

All About Rain Gardens. (n.d.). Groundwater Foundation. https://www.groundwater.org/action/ home/raingardens.html

All images are courtesy of Pixabay.

Animal. (n.d.). Planet Natural Research Center. https:// www.planetnatural.com/pest-problem-solver/lawn-pests/animal-control/

Barton, R. (2013, June 6). *Know Your Garden Soil: How to Make the Most of Your Soil Type.* Eartheasy. https://learn.

eartheasy.com/articles/know-your-garden-soil-how-to-make-the-most-of-your-soil-type/

BH&G Garden Editors. (2020a, June 1). *How to Understand Your Yard's Sunlight So You Know What to Plant Where.* Better Homes & Gardens. https://www.bhg.com/gardening/how-to-garden/understanding-your-yard-s-sunlight/

BH&G Garden Editors. (2020b, September 14). *How to Use Hardiness Zone Information to Figure Out What You Can Grow.* Better Homes & Gardens. https://www.bhg.com/gardening/gardening-by-region/how-to-use-hardiness-zone-information/

Childs, J. (2018, August 2). *7 Common Garden Diseases.* Garden Gate. https://www.gardengatemagazine.com/articles/how-to/deal-with-pests/seven-common-garden-diseases/

Composting At Home. (2021). United States Environmental Protection Agency [EPA]. https://www.epa.gov/recycle/composting-home

Controlling Pests on Flowers, Roses & Ornamental Plants. (n.d.). Ortho. https://www.ortho.com/en-us/library/garden/controlling-pests-flowers-roses-ornamental-plants

Ellis, M. E. (2021, July 23). *Flower Spacing Guide: Learn About Spacing Flowering Plants.* Gardening Know How. https://www.gardeningknowhow.com/ornamental/flowers/fgen/flower-spacing-guide.htm

Fertilizing Flower Garden Plants. (2021, May 14). University of Massachusetts Amherst. https://ag.umass.edu/home-lawn-garden/fact-sheets/fertilizing-flower-garden-plants

Gardenia. (2021). *Hardiness Zones / 12.* Gardenia. https://www.gardenia.net/plants/hardiness-zones/12

Gardenia. (2021). *Hardiness Zones / 13.* Gardenia. https://www.gardenia.net/plants/hardiness-zones/13

Garrity, A. (2020, May 29). *20 of the Best Perennial Flowers and Plants That'll Bloom Year After Year.* Good Housekeeping. https://www.goodhousekeeping.com/home/gardening/g32673850/best-perennial-flowers-plants/?slide=1

GIM_Team. (2015, August 20). *The All-In-One, Square Foot Gardening Plant Spacing Guide w/ Printable Chart (60+ Plants!).* Garden In Minutes. https://gardeninminutes.com/plant-spacing-chart-raised-bed-gardening/

Hagen, L. (n.d.). *How & When To Plant Bulbs.* Garden Design. https://www.gardendesign.com/bulbs/how-to.html

Helmenstine, A. M. (2020, January 24). *How to Make a Red Cabbage pH Indicator*. ThoughtCo. https://www. thoughtco.com/making-red-cabbage-ph-indicator-603650

How to Build a French Drain. (2011). Deep Green Permaculture. https://deepgreenpermaculture.com/diy-instructions/how-to-build-a-french-drain/

How to Determine the Best Sun Exposure for Your Garden. (2018, December 20). My Little Green Garden. https://mylittlegreengarden.com/sun-exposure-for-your-garden/

How To Use A Soil pH Test Kit. (2014, January 8). Enjoy Your Garden. https://www.enjoy-your-garden.com/garden-soil.html

Iannotti, M. (2020, September 17). *How to Conduct a Soil pH Test*. The Spruce. https://www.thespruce.com/do-it-yourself-soil-ph-test-4125833

Irrigation Methods. (n.d.). Extension: University of Missouri. https://extension.missouri.edu/programs/irrigation/irrigation-system-pros-and-cons

Isleib, J. (2012, December 19). *Signs and symptoms of plant disease: Is it fungal, viral or bacterial?* Michigan State University Extension. https://www.canr.msu.edu/

news/signs_and_symptoms_of_plant_disease_is_it_fu
ngal_viral_or_bacterial

Martin, K. (2020, February 5). *10 Best Wind Tolerant Flowers*. Urban Garden Gal. https://www.urbangardengal.com/wind-tolerant-flowers/

Martin, S. (2019, July 22). *Seven Essential Summer Gardening Tasks*. Garden Crossings. https://www.gardencrossings.com/blog/seven-essential-summer-gardening-tasks/

Martin, S. (n.d.-a). *10 Essential Spring Gardening Tasks*. Proven Winners. https://www.provenwinners.com/learn/early-spring/10-essential-spring-gardening-tasks

Martin, S. (n.d.-b). *10 Tasks to Keep Your Summer Garden Singing*. Proven Winners. https://www.provenwinners.com/learn/soil/10-tasks-keep-your-summer-garden-singing

Meyer, K. (2021). *Zoning in on Hardiness*. Proven Winners. https://www.provenwinners.com/learn/zoning-hardiness

Mlgardener. (n.d.). *5 Simple Ingredients to Fix Poor Draining Soil*. Mlgardener. https://migardener.com/5-simple-ingredients-to-fix-poor-draining-soil/

MorningChores Staff. (n.d.). *5 Best Insecticides to Eliminate Bugs, Ants, and Pests in Your Garden.* Morning Chores. https://morningchores.com/best-insecticides/

Plant Diseases. (n.d.). Planet Natural Research Center. https://www.planetnatural.com/pest-problem-solver/plant-disease/

Thompson, D. (n.d.). *Garden Irrigation Techniques.* SFGate. https://homeguides.sfgate.com/garden-irrigation-techniques-75132.html

Tilley, N. (2021, July 26). *Wind Resistant Plants For Gardens.* Gardening Know How. https://www.gardeningknowhow.com/special/spaces/wind-resistant-plants-for-your-windy-garden.htm

USDA Plant Hardiness Map. (n.d.). USDA. https://planthardiness.ars.usda.gov/

Vinje E. (2013). *Home Composting 101.* Plant Natural Research Center. https://www.planetnatural.com/home-composting/

West Coast Garden. (2019, November 20). *Your Winter Garden Cleanup Checklist.* West Coast Gardens. https://westcoastgardens.ca/our-resources/your-winter-garden-cleanup-checklist